"Trina's soul is not unlike her innate design sense. It's deep and searching, forever shifting to make room, to carve space, to find a new purpose for it all—the hardship and shiplap, the mundane and the mirror, the strife and the sofa. What a beautiful gift it is to witness such transformations in her living room and living heart."

—Erin Loechner, founder of DesignforMankind.com and author of *Chasing Slow*

"Every inch of this book—the images, the words, and Trina's story of losing and finding—is a call to consider how beauty heals us. Not the slick, glossy pretty of perfect worlds. But the hard-won beauty of everyday loving and living. Maybe most of all, these pages remind us of hope we all need to hear: that even life's endings can become beautiful beginnings in God's hands."

—Leeana Tankersley, author of *Begin Again*

"Trina wears her heart on her sleeve—and for that I'm grateful. Her message of grace overcoming loss is a gift to all of us. The heartfelt honesty on these pages will meet you like an old friend."

—Gabe Lyons, President, *Q* and author of *Good Faith*

"Trina McNeilly views the unswept corners of life through the persistent gaze of beauty and the outcome is contagious. With the eye of a designer, the soul of a poet, and the compassion of a daughter deeply loved by God, Trina helps us bring order to our hearts along with our living rooms. Fun, warm, and vulnerable to the core, I devoured this book."

—Shannan Martin, author of *Falling Free: Rescued From the Life I Always Wanted*

"I've experienced a tragedy that left me with more questions than hope, wanting to close down my heart and stop searching for truth. For me, turning the corner on events like this come from thoughtful and vulnerable discussion with others. That is what I experience from Trina's book—heartfelt and honest storytelling that helps me deeply reflect and inch closer to truth."

—Barrett Ward, CEO/founder of ABLE

"Trina will challenge you to believe that endings are beginnings and that something beautiful can be built out of the ruins of your brokenness. This book will leave you believing that nothing in your life is wasted…every part of your story has potential to burst with purpose."

—Tracy Wilde, author and speaker,
Finding the Lost Art of Empathy

"Trina articulates how design, done properly, can be a manifestation of our intentions about how we want to live. She cuts straight through the superficial and focuses on the beauty of the heart. Her book is a must read for anyone looking to live intentionally and with love."

—Kirsten Grove, interior stylist and author

La La lovely.

THE ART OF FINDING BEAUTY IN THE EVERYDAY

TRINA MCNEILLY

FaithWords

New York   Nashville

FaithWords
Hachette Book Group
1290 Avenue of the Americas, New York, NY 10104
faithwords.com
twitter.com/faithwords

First Edition: April 2018

FaithWords is a division of Hachette Book Group, Inc. The FaithWords name and logo are trademarks of Hachette Book Group, Inc.

The publisher is not responsible for websites (or their content) that are not owned by the publisher.

The Hachette Speakers Bureau provides a wide range of authors for speaking events. To find out more, go to www.hachettespeakersbureau.com or call (866) 376-6591.

Print book interior design by Camby Designs

Library of Congress Cataloging-in-Publication Data

Library of Congress Control Number: 2017959279

ISBNs: 978-1-4789-2076-2 (hardcover); 978-1-4789-2077-9 (eBook)

Printed in Canada

FRI

10 9 8 7 6 5 4 3 2 1

To the ones who have offered and
exemplified true beauty in my life.

In memory of:
Hilda Tompkins, my grandma
The beauty of wisdom and hope

For:
Cynthia Tompkins, my mom
The beauty of grace and selfless love

Amy Tompkins, my sister
The beauty of creativity and dreaming

Ella McNeilly, my daughter
The beauty of being a beloved daughter
who has found her voice and uses it

"The sweetest thing in all my life has been the longing...
to find the place where all beauty came from."

—C. S. LEWIS, *TILL WE HAVE FACES*

TABLE OF CONTENTS

Everyone needs a friend like Trina. I've known this gem for twenty years. She's my go-to girl on all things fashion, makeup, jewelry, denim, and, yes, I even FaceTimed her when picking out a living room chandelier. We've trekked through London in the rain, decorated my New York apartment for a Land of Nod photo shoot, shared a favorite author—Andrew Murray—and learned how to make meringue. I still haven't mastered that last one, to be honest.

She is everything she says she is. There's no pomp and circumstance, no overembellishment, no voice of bravado. Instead, Trina's words are a gentle hug, or "hygge" as she describes on page 320. They comfort and console, dripping with wisdom, the fruit of finding beauty in the rubble.

She's helped me dig through my own rubble.

A few years ago during a season of panic attacks, Trina texted me these words out of the blue:

I'll give you a full life in the emptiest of places—firm

muscles, strong bones. You'll be like a well-watered gar-
den, a gurgling spring that never runs dry. You'll use the old
rubble of past lives to build anew, rebuild the foundations
from out of your past. You'll be known as those who can fix
anything, restore old ruins, rebuild and renovate, make the
community livable again. Isaiah 58 MSG

For most of us, there comes a moment where we face the sting of heartache, rejection, or pain. For some, the memories are loud and literal; for others, the reminders are subtle—or, worse, silent. In response, we numb out, point fingers, or sometimes both. If only it were that simple. But blame cannot be acutely named. There are always more layers to the story.

Nevertheless, we unravel.

Perhaps you've lost love, legacy, or hope. There is nothing so ugly it cannot be beautiful. There is nothing so wounded it cannot be healed. There is nothing so painful you cannot recover. There is nothing so lost it cannot be found.

When you unravel, you always rebuild.

When life strays from the dandelion wishes of our youth, Trina helps us answer the question "How do we respond?" She leads us on a scavenger hunt for the loveliest of survivors, determined to find redemption in the ruin. The wisdom found here is chock-full of beauty and grace, redemption and restoration. I cried precious tears of remembrance of God's faithfulness page after page. What a comfort to know our Father in heaven—*Love* Himself—always protects, trusts, hopes, and perseveres.

Survivors make the most beautiful people. They know where they've been, where they're headed, and, most importantly, that they're loved. And like Trina, they know how to lead others—people like you and me—forward.

Rebekah Lyons
Author, *You Are Free* and *Freefall to Fly*

beautif
spaces
broken

ul
and
places

"Sometimes beauty is so deep it pierces us with longing. For what? For life as it was meant to be. Beauty reminds us of an Eden we have never known, but somehow know our hearts were created for. Beauty speaks of heaven to come, when all shall be beautiful. It haunts us with eternity."

—JOHN AND STASI ELDREDGE, *CAPTIVATING*[1]

I have this habit of looking for the lovely. Some days I find it in perfectly styled spaces, and other days I find it in the broken places.

Some days I do the finding, and other days beauty finds me. And during the long dark winters, where I live just northwest of Chicago, it's more like mining. It's digging. It's discovering. But no matter the day or season, beauty is there just waiting to be found. To be noticed. To be uncovered.

It's not beyond the laundry pile, chipped paint, dirty dishes, broken table, or broken life. It's right in the center of it.

There is beauty in your green toile patterned plates crusted over with last night's spaghetti dinner. There is beauty in the white paint peeling off the side of the house that you can't afford to have fixed. There is beauty stuffed between the mountains of sweaty socks and stained shirts on your laundry room floor. Yes, there is even beauty to be found in your broken life that shows no promise of being put together again.

I've always had an eye for beautiful things. I just never knew it. I called it good taste. I inherited it from my parents, who exemplified class. My little sister, Amy, is the creative one in my family. The baby. The free spirit. The one who graduated from the Art Institute of Chicago. I'm the oldest, the predictable one who plays by the rules and makes a lot of plans. The one who prides herself on, and is weighed down by, responsibility. The one others assume has it all figured out. The opposite end of the spectrum. It was my sister who taught me that we are all creative. Every one of us. How could we not be? We are children of the Creator. Over time, I slowly began to believe that, yes, I did, in fact, have an eye for finding beauty and that it was inherent. This ability to find and create beauty is an attribute that the Creator wove into each and every one of us. Beauty points us to God, and expressing it points others to Him.

When I began blogging ten years ago, I didn't have a goal or endgame. I had simply found a place to share—my words, imagery, ideas, inspiration, information, and life. My blog was a place to collect all of my gatherings. At the time, I had two little ones and spent most of my time at home. And as it turned out, that is where I found beauty—in things that pertained to the home. It was practical, and it became my pattern to collect and catalog images that I found beautiful.

Eventually, I began sharing images of my own home. Photos of my perfectly imperfect life were pinned and re-pinned. Rooms that were perfectly styled spaces. But behind the photo was real life, of course. Crying kids who didn't want to comply. Messy piles pushed aside in another room. And a broken heart that no pretty picture could crop out.

While I spent my days sharing beauty, redecorating my home, looking for lovely things, and sharing my finds, home as I had always known it fell apart. Just shy of forty years of marriage, my parents got divorced. It shocked me and shattered my heart. To complicate the matter, I live in my childhood home, which is a museum of memories. It has been six very long years of grieving. Grieving family. Grieving what once was. Grieving what could have been. I had never truly had my heart broken, and I never suspected that someone else's breakup could break me. But it can. It did.

I found it ironic, almost cruel, that I would have to journey through this dismantling of home in the very place where my *definition* of home was first defined.

The first year of the divorce process, I couldn't even tell you that I was broken. I knew my family was fractured; however, I didn't realize I was. It took a friend telling me that I had a broken heart. She named it, connecting the physical and emotional like numbered dots in a coloring book, and gave me permission to stop pretending that I was OK when I was not.

I carried a newborn in my arms, an eighteen-month-old on my hip, and on my shoulders the weight of the unknown. (*How will this all play out? Will my parents really go through with a divorce? Will this change everything? Will my relationship with my parents stay the same? Will they create new lives? How would I fit within their new lives? Will my mom be OK? Will my dad be OK? What can I do to make it better? Will all they have built crumble? Will anything remain the same?*) To cope, I spent uncounted hours letting myself get lost in La La Lovely land. I diverted my attention from the storm around me, and the one inside me, by way of a blue-lit screen. I searched beautiful spaces, took virtual home tours, visited faraway cities by a click of the mouse, conversed with new blog friends, and sometimes partook in retail therapy, purchasing pretty things for a short-lived pick-me-up.

Many days I sought comfort in the computer over God's word. For the first time in my life, I felt as if He was distant. I felt let down by my parents and by God. The ground was suddenly shaky; the clear view became cloudy.

Yet it was while I was trying to get lost in the lovely—avoiding my pain and sometimes, even, God—that Beauty Himself found me. Psalm 100:5 tells us that "God *is* sheer beauty, all-generous in love, loyal always and ever" (MSG, emphasis added).

This *all*-generous-love, loyal *always and ever* God stuck by my side. My angry side. My good side. My depressed side. My unlovely side. Even my side that questioned Him. This is the greatest beauty I have ever known: a God who tenderly loves the unlovely. It was this relentless love that gave me eyes to see beauty in the middle of the busy, messy, broken everyday.

———— ....

Many of us have a bad taste in our mouths regarding beauty, as though it's a forbidden thing—frivolous and fading. But beauty was at the beginning. Beauty is the beginning. God *is* beauty. And His creation is a tangible beauty that is taken in with all of our senses. Yet I'm struck still when I recall that the greatest expression of beauty is humanity. Made in His image. Made in the image of sheer beauty. You and I.

If we are made in the image of beauty personified, then I can't believe it to be frivolous or fading. I see it as eternal, original, and good just as God said it was good (Gen. 1:27, 31 AMP).

I believe all these centuries later, far beyond Eden, He is saying, "Look, it is so good. Look, I AM so very good. If you really look, Beloved, beauty is not beyond the mundane or broken."

EVERY HARDSHIP, EACH NEGATIVE CIRCUMSTANCE, AND ALL BROKENNESS IS AN OPPORTUNITY TO FIND MORE OF GOD. WHICH, IN TURN, MEANS TO FIND MORE BEAUTY.

God asks us to look for, discover, and uncover the beauty in His perfect creation (and some days He even asks us to add to it in our own unique and artistic way). For when we find beauty, we find God.

Every hardship, each negative circumstance, and all brokenness is an opportunity to find more of God. Which, in turn, means to find more beauty.

In this series of essays, I'll share stories and inspiration from my journey of finding, and being found by, beauty. You will find beauty among the broken, as I share deep matters of the heart along with practical pointers on things like decorating your home, finding your style, and creating beautiful spaces.

Let's get to finding; it's an art that doesn't require a special skill set. More than that, let's allow ourselves to be found. As you awaken to the art of finding beauty in the everyday, you will begin to see life through the eyes of the One who saw light when there was only darkness, and this changes everything.

PART ONE

CHAPTER ONE | THE OFFERING OF BEAUTY

ONE

"*Here is the simple truth I keep trying to own,
the one that breaks the bounds of beauty;
everything is in God and God is in everything.*"

—SUE MONK KIDD, *FIRSTLIGHT, THE EARLY INSPIRATIONAL WRITINGS*[1]

G ood morning,

This is Beauty. I want you to notice me, to not look past me, to not feel shame for indulging in me, to not strive for me, to not dull me down, to not agree with the lie that I am unnecessary or frivolous, to not believe me to be a thing only of your past or far off in your future. I am present in all days.

I am mountains. I am sea. I am flowers. I am trees. I am a child's laugh, a grandmother's hug, and a sandwich shared with a friend. I am ears that listen, a kind word spoken, a cup of cold water given. I am a song to comfort and a song to dance to. I am bright colors and calming white. I am savory, and I am sweet. I'm a walk outside when your life feels suffocating. I'm a crackling fire on a bitter winter's day. I am the plump rolls on a baby's legs and the grooves of life etched like artwork on a ninety-two-year-old's face. I am nature. I am art. I am a grand gesture and a quiet acknowledgment, all the same. I am inside. I am outside. I'm a hushed whisper and a shout through a megaphone seeking your attention. On Tuesday, I'm a sunset, and on Thursday, I'm the pattern made in the leaves scattered on the street. I am a first kiss, a last kiss, and all the kisses in between. I am tears that fall like rain, in grief, collected and counted (Ps. 56:8 MSG). I am all shapes, sizes, colors, sounds, and sights. I'll pursue like a groom, and I wait like a sage. I am an offering of heaven come down.

They say beauty is in the eye of the beholder.

I wonder, *What do you see?*

Are you beholding?

Blinded by beauty?

Or blinded *to* beauty?

———————————— · · · ·

Not so long ago, a significant voice in my life told me to stop living in La La Land. Humorous and hurtful all at once, I'm certain the person who said it meant all the pun that puddled out of their mouth when they spoke those words.

I laughed at the childlike dig until I realized a day later that the words had dug right down into the soil of my heart. They were seeds that took root in my brokenness. And I knew they were seeds I did not want to sprout.

Were my blog, projects, and online life simply distractions? A diversion from my pain? An escape from my reality? A place to get lost when I needed to be found? The truth is that I took to my computer many nights like some throw back the extra glass of wine. My eyes bloodshot, glazed over, after pinning and posting until two a.m. My life felt so completely out of control, but online I could create order. In real life, I felt confined in my home and imprisoned in my pain, but on my blog I could make space. I made money, but not quite enough to call it a career. I had no endgame or business plan. I didn't believe I could call myself an entrepreneur or even a girl with a goal. I had a few accomplishments I was really proud of: mentioned in the *New York Times*; published in The Land of Nod catalog for styling my home and my friend's New York City apartment; featured in Design Mom's *New York Times*–bestselling book.

Maybe I do live in La La Land? My very own non-reality. My very own online Eden, that transported me far from the reality of my broken, no longer idyllic home. I swam in the puddle of that person's words for a while.

I unabashedly confess that, many times, it was my digital distraction. However, as time went on, it also became a place where I shared heartache, processed pain, and offered hope as I began to feel it in my flesh again.

Now, "La La Land" is both endearing and partly true. It was

(and is) a place for me. A place for me to show up and write, even if some days it was only about couches and color and cast-iron cookie recipes; I was still writing. I practiced within the parameters of my purpose and my gifting. I found and used my voice. It was also a place in which I found community among fellow seekers, who, like me, were looking for something. Perhaps they, too, were searching for beauty in the midst of their brokenness, much like the Israelites who looked for a place to rest in the desert and were met with God's grace (Jer. 31:2 MSG).

TO FIND BEAUTY WITHIN THE BROKEN IS TO BEHOLD, "TO KEEP AND REMEMBER," THE GOODNESS OF GOD.

I'm not saying that the Internet or blogging are places of rest. I found both tiring and taxing over time. They were the avenues, however, to my awakening to beauty, expanding my views and teaching me to behold beauty and to be held by Beauty.

Beauty is not an escape. It is an answer.

Beauty is not a distraction. It is our focal point. To turn our eyes from our problems, what plagues us, and our broken world and to focus in on beauty—the small gifts and unnoticed grand gestures—is the answer. To behold something is to see it and hold it in your attention.[2] *Behold* derives from the old English word *Behealden*, meaning "to hold, have, preserve, belong, gaze upon, consider, keep." In fact, "keep" is the consistent etymology in many languages.

BEAUTY IS GOD'S
ULTIMATE FORM OF
HOSPITALITY TOWARD
US: JUST TO BEHOLD.
BECAUSE THAT IS A
VALUE OF HIS: TO
BEHOLD BEAUTIFUL
THINGS.

In German, it is "to keep and remember."[3] To find beauty within the broken is to behold, "to keep and remember," the goodness of God.

Beauty is our answer because God is our answer. And God, in His great goodness, offered beauty to us at the beginning when he offered us Himself.

In Cape Town, where the Indian and Atlantic Oceans swell together and compete with Table Mountain's majesty, some of the world's most palpable brokenness is in residence. The calming ocean and exalted mountains encircle countless victims of human trafficking and modern-day slavery. My friend Christina lives within this juxtaposition of beauty and brokenness.

We Vox back and forth, Christina and I. We send each other eleven-minute-long messages that cross the seas from South Africa to America. We talk about home, the landscape she lives in, the years she spent fighting human trafficking. We talk about travel, food, spiritual practices, forgiveness, and the healing journey we both are on. So different, yet the same. Christina is a trusted friend, a sounding board in step with the Spirit. She listens to me better than I listen to myself.

When I was processing this book idea, she left me a Vox, and somewhere sandwiched between what she'd been eating and where she'd been riding her bike while visiting Amsterdam, she shared why she found beauty necessary:

"We have to accept beauty for beauty. It neither needs to be useful nor a means to an end. God created this world for us. Beauty is God's ultimate form of hospitality toward us: just to behold. Because that is a value of His: to behold beautiful things."

Beauty is God's holy offering to us: an offering of heaven come down to earth. The grandeur of this earth is but a glimpse of God Himself and our heavenly home. Surely, then, beauty is not an indulgence but a necessity. To not accept this offering and to live a life with eyes, hands, and hearts shut tight is to live an empty, impoverished life.

Beauty is God's artwork, His creation, whose purpose is to echo and reflect the very color and light of His kingdom on this earth—no more superfluous than you or I. We are the beauty of God *in* a broken world.

Open your eyes

This is the beginning of beholding.

Don't look past the nature outside your front door. Find a handsome object in a room. Mountains of majesty surrounding war-torn towns. A half-moon smile worn by a sick child, exposing a well of joy. Food bubbling on the stove, infusing the air with a comfort that masks your messy, out-of-order house. A kind word that quenches like a cup of cold water on a hot day. The bright color of her coat. The warm touch of his hand. The poems you picked back up and the new ones that began to pour out of your soul.

I wonder what form of beauty you, at one time, noticed, dabbled in, or enjoyed. Why did you stop? Perhaps someone called it a waste of time. Maybe it was a direct word from a weighty one in your life. Maybe it was a sarcastic look from a stranger. Maybe it was your own voice that shut you up or shut you down. Whichever it was, you put down the pen, you let the paintbrushes dry out, you closed your eyes and your life.

Open your heart

This is where Beauty lives, where He makes His home.

Consider this: perhaps, like me, the beauty you are to behold (to consider) is within the parameters of your purpose, your gifting that was embroidered into the very fibers of your being (Ps. 139:15 AMP). Beholding could very well be the beginning of your practice, leading to purpose and eventually to the place that you'll find you fit like a puzzle. It is time to start practicing again.

Open your hands

This is how beauty is transferred from one to another.

This is the offering from Him to you and from you to others.

And so the offering never ends.

———— ....

01 /   What did beauty look like to you before you were blinded by brokenness? Before life clouded your view and sucked out the color?

02 /   Go outside. Close your eyes. Take a deep breath, in and out, and then open your eyes. What do you see? What do you hear? What do you feel? Write down what beauty you behold.

03 /   Pray this prayer: "Father, open my heart to You, to the beauty You've created for me to behold as well as the beauty You wove within me. I receive this offering from heaven. Beauty is not beyond brokenness or the ordinary everyday but right within it. I pray that You would guide me in the offering that I'm to give and that ultimately I'd be a conduit and reflection of Your radiant beauty to this earth."

CHAPTER TWO | THE END IS THE BEGINNING

TWO

hat feels like the end is often the beginning. I haven't always seen it that way, though.

Ends were ends, and beginnings were starts. And from my start, I dreamed up beginnings and spent a lot of my days planning for tomorrows. I painted them bright and expected them to shine a bit brighter than what my imagination drew up. I watched my father create goals and then draw up meticulous strategies to execute his red-pen plans. Eventually those plans became colored pushpins on a map representing newspapers he purchased across the country. Naturally, I believed if I could dream it, I could accomplish anything too. I dreamed of a husband, a family of my own, a career in ministry *and* the family newspaper business, a cozy home, and a golden retriever to boot. Part dreamer and always a planner, I find that I am most comfortable living in the middles and mapping out the starts. The ends, for me, always seem uncertain and endlessly far away.

But sometimes ends come unexpectedly, regardless of plans made for the middles. I learned this one spring as I was bringing my fourth baby into the world and as my grandfather was leaving it.

Seasons are a beautiful example of endings turning into beginnings, and as it was, winter was wandering into spring. The flowers began to grow bright and beautiful in the warm sun. My heart, in reverse, started growing cold. My beloved grandpa was dying, and I wasn't ready to let go. Out my window, winter was coming to an end; inside, it was the beginning of an almost endless winter for me. Only a couple of months prior, my dad told me that he and my mom were divorcing. In his best business voice, he informed me that it would likely be a lengthy process. I lived in the tension of no definite end and hoping it wouldn't really happen. I held on to the words of Rilke: "For among these winters there is one so endlessly winter that only by wintering through it will your heart survive."[2]

The tulips, the ones that returned each year like grandparents at Christmastime, began to decorate our yard with ruby reds and sunshine yellows. My little ones and I would stand over the first of the flowers, and I'd tell them a tale of fairies making their homes in these Dutch tulips. Like an adoring mother, the red and yellow flowers would tuck the fairies in each night as they closed to the darkness; and each morning, like a yawn, they would open to the kiss of the sun that set them free.

I wished I had the energy to mother like that, or better yet, I wished I were a cocooned fairy who could fly away each day. I was starting to grieve the past along with the future memories I felt were being taken from me.

Life and death.

Beginning and end.

That year, the spring air was thick with it.

Days before my fourth child was born, I had a long look into my grandpa's steel baby blues. Tracing past his lines, I saw a look about him that was unsettling. Always the handsome one, even he couldn't hide that he was fading. He stared into my eyes for a very long time, almost to the point of me being uncomfortable. It was as if he was reading my soul. Tracing my times. Imprinting an image on his heart. Recording. Logging. Keeping a vision of me until we met again. He looked at me, line by line, and I wondered if he could read my pain. Could he feel it, like Braille, when he held my hand? We kept my parents' divorce from him, but I was certain he saw my sorrow that day. When he finally spoke, he said, "You know I love you."

"Yes, I know you do," I whispered.

"My, you look just like your mother," he said after a pause.

I knew he meant some kind of similarity that went far beyond the moon-shaped eyes we share. I wrapped my arms around him and told him how very much I loved him and said a few other things that needed saying. I kissed his tired, gentle face and wondered if it would be the last time. It felt like a final goodbye. I left his house praying begging, bargaining prayers that it was not.

I couldn't catch my breath after that. I drove the short distance home, walked through the kitchen, right past my little ones, to the back office and began gasping. I sobbed, trying to swallow air that was too thick to go down. *I can't breathe! I can't breathe! I can't breathe!* I repeated this over and over again.

Endings are imminent. Even the beginning I was about to birth made me short of breath. What if I couldn't focus on new life because I was rocking too many endings?

Gasping for air, I wondered where in the world God was. I had always felt so close to Him, and suddenly I felt so far. The harshness of life felt like it was creating some kind of continental divide.

EVEN THE BEGINNING I WAS ABOUT TO BIRTH MADE ME SHORT OF BREATH. WHAT IF I COULDN'T FOCUS ON NEW LIFE BECAUSE I WAS ROCKING TOO MANY ENDINGS?

I didn't feel like doing what I knew to do, but I picked up my Bible anyway, hoping for hope to find me. And, right there in front of me, without looking, searching, flipping, or finding, God gently reminded me with these words that He had gone nowhere:

"True to your word, You let me *catch my breath* and send me in the right direction" (Ps. 23:3 MSG, emphasis mine).

I wasn't sure how He'd let me catch my breath. But I was certain *He knew* I needed catching. His ears were tuned to the sound of my sighing. He'd let me catch my breath. For "God keeps an eye on his friends, his ears pick up every moan and groan" (Ps. 34:15 MSG). He heard my prayer, my cry for help.

I WASN'T SURE HOW HE'D LET ME CATCH MY BREATH. BUT I WAS CERTAIN *HE KNEW* I NEEDED CATCHING.

I waited on a breath of heaven.

Days later, my fourth child was born. A beginning. New life, with the fresh scent of heaven. We named him Rockwell Royal (we call him Rocco), which means "rest" and "of the King." Every time I whispered his name I was declaring "rest from heaven."

My grandpa lived two more months and passed the day before my thirty-fourth birthday. I was by his side when he took his very last breath on earth, which I knew was immediately followed by his first eternal breath. It was a sacred moment.

In two short months, I witnessed one coming from heaven

and one going. One taking their first breath and the other breathing their last. One bringing the tangible breath of heaven to earth and the other letting go of theirs to enter eternity. Holy moments. Life and death are not so far apart. Both connected by breath and the home of heaven.

One coming.

One going.

Beginnings and endings.

I nursed new life and carried tiny Rest from Heaven in my tired arms. I did my best to process my grandpa's passing. To accept that *goodbye* was for good on this side of eternity. I wouldn't be picking up bologna and cheese for him at the deli or popping over for a quick visit on my way back from dropping off the kids at school. Every time I made a roast, baked peanut butter cookies, or took my tea with one spoonful of sugar, I couldn't share it with him. I had to let go of yet another form of security, a pillar and protector in my life. My grandpa's name was Warren, which means "protecting friend," and that is exactly who he was in my life. The last thing I gave him was a friendship bracelet.

I managed on a new mom's adrenaline but began to crash daily when I tried to accept the impending death of my family by way of my parents' divorce.

Over the next year as Rocco grew and giggled, something in me shrank. Hope died a slow death without me noticing until it was too late. And just like that, a cloud passed over my life and took up residence in my heart. A storm cloud that carried great pressure. I felt this slow process of breaking within as well as the breaking all around.

I slowly came undone—it was a process. Breaking. Broken. Broke. This wasn't a clean break, mind you. It was jagged and painful. A crack, smash, a tear, an unweaving, a hanging by a thread until the tiny thread severs, unties, or snaps in two. It was an undoing of who I was and who I thought I was, what I thought life was and how it was always supposed to be.

I wondered if I'd ever be whole again. If all that was familiar would be lost. Would I ever be *me* again? Or just frays and fragments of myself? Maybe things could be taped up. Tied up. Pieced together again. Enough to function. Enough to feel. But healed and whole? For the first time in my life, I doubted it. I had always been optimistic, sure that anything could be fixed and over time get better. It was easy to believe this for others. Not so much for myself. I was starting to think that maybe scars and breaks were just what we wore after we lived life and life lived all over us.

I spent months whispering desolate prayers like "Help!" "Jesus." "Oh God." "Please." The kinds of prayers that sounded more like sighs or breathing. I didn't understand it at the time, but He was helping me catch my breath. He *was* my very breath.

This breath that starts our beginnings and ushers us into our endings is also very much in our middles. In the living, day in and day out—the everyday.

Breathe in.

Breathe out.

We don't notice the melodic rhythm of it on our good days, and we gasp and gulp for it on our worst days. But His breath is there; we are made of it. Genesis 2:7 says, "God formed man out of dirt from the ground and blew into his nostrils the breath of life. The man came alive—a living soul" (MSG).

"I live and breathe God" (Ps. 34:2 MSG) because He lives in me.

WITH EVERY ENDING, GOD IS AUTHORING
A BEGINNING. OUR CURRENT FAILURES ARE
BEING WRITTEN INTO FUTURE OPPORTUNITIES.

These days I try to pay attention to my breath—sometimes with the help of yoga or a reminder on my Apple Watch. But mostly I listen to the whisper from within that reminds me that He is the very air I breathe. Since that day with my grandpa, nearly six years ago, I have had more than my share of times where I've been frantic, panicked, short of breath, or overcome with anxiety. And each time the only way through has been to breathe.

Every exhale followed by an inhale.

Every ending followed by a beginning.

Every death followed by new life.

Beauty begins in the letting go.

If you are struggling through an ending

01 / Exhale. Let it all out. Don't hold anything back. Remember, God's ears pick up every moan and groan.

02 / Think about this: the end of what you thought could be perfect is the beginning of beauty. Ecclesiastes 7:8 tells us, "Endings are better than beginnings..." (MSG).

03 / With every ending, God is authoring a beginning. Our current failures are being written into future opportunities. He takes what breaks us and builds a new foundation.

04 / Inhale. Breathe it all in. The possibility of change. The permission to dream. The hope that will carry you.

what feels like
the End
is often
the Beginning

the lan of a br heart

CHAPTER THREE | THE LANDSCAPE OF A BROKEN HEART

THREE

"Go to your bosom:
Knock there, and ask your
heart what it doth know."

—WILLIAM SHAKESPEARE, *MEASURE FOR MEASURE*[1]

I want to help you find beauty. To wake you up to the promise of beauty finding you. It's likely that you don't have to look very far to find hurt or pain in your life. It's possible that it is prevalent, that it's bubbling up and over like green beans you forgot were boiling on the stove. Or it may be that you've tuned out the ache like a staticky station on the radio. And no matter how many times you hit the Scan button, the station it lands on has the background buzz behind the music.

Many of us have found a way to walk away from the stove, busying and distracting ourselves with every other thing.

We've turned the burner down to a simmer so that we can multitask, returning to the pot every so often, adding water, feeding the boil so the beans don't burn. If this is how you are handling hurt or pain, then you are not handling it at all. You are managing it. You are coping.

If you've tuned out the ache and trained your ears to ignore the static, then chances are you are tone-deaf to the state of your heart.

I spent many years scanning stations and ignoring the static. I was unable to tune into any one station long enough to hear what was playing in the background. Yet when my world shifted, so did my focus. The station went completely static. So I turned off the radio.

I didn't realize the real problem was that I had a broken heart. I'd never experienced anything like this before. The closest I had come was my so-called heartbreak over a high school boyfriend.

Pain, for me, had always been a very private thing. And in the midst of this fresh pain, I couldn't put a sentence together to describe the storm inside me. I couldn't even spit out the words, "My parents are getting a divorce," to some of my oldest and dearest friends. I rehearsed telling them, in my head, over and over. Like a child, I felt like if I didn't say it out loud, it wasn't true. I was so raw that to say the words was like ripping off the bandage I was using not to protect the wound but to hide its ugliness.

Then someone gave language to what I couldn't express. I hope to do that for you.

I fought brokenness as most people do. We are taught to keep it *all* together. Certainly that pertains to our hearts too. I've handled hurt and pain my whole life. Yes, it got to me, but I kept going like one of my favorite '80s songs, "Ain't Nothing Gonna Break My Stride" by Joe Ferry and the Big Ska Band.[2]

I would slow down for a day or two, but I'd always keep moving. Because that is what a good responsible person does. Especially a responsible Christian girl. There is work to be done. There is a world to save. There is life to live. And, after all, there are still things to be grateful for. "Keep calm and carry on," like the mugs and the T-shirts and the framed poster on my wall say. That's exactly it: you move along with all that you carry. Until you can no longer bear what you've been holding.

Then one day you wake up, and it's a seemingly normal day, only it isn't because it's the day that alters everything, forever. It's the day you can't take back. And from here on out you think about strange and stupid things like the probability of time travel. You cry when Cher comes on the radio singing "If I Could Turn Back Time." And you cry, again, when you can't get the stupid song out of your head. The day that changes everything can come by way of a choice you made, a choice someone else made, or an accident.

When that day comes, the one thing you find you can't do—no matter how well you've done it over the years—is move. You do the opposite. You freeze. You feel suspended in time. The hands of time seem to take you back only to yesterdays or into hypothetical tomorrows. The place you are most afraid to be is in today.

I was in my laundry room when time stopped—when I received the phone call informing me of the divorce. I can't remember if I was switching a load or looking for a lost sock, but from that moment on, I watched my childhood play over and over in my head, as if I were binge-watching a series on Netflix. I looked for evidence and tried to create a case for my parents' divorce like I was Miss Marple. I acted out scenes in my head of Christmases to come. I fixated on the fact that two of my children would know Gommy and Papa together and two would not. Everything became a "last," and I did not want to imagine all of the soon-coming "firsts." Last trip to Tucson. First Christmas Eve not together. Eventually, I played the past over and over like beloved reruns of *Friends* and *Frasier*. When I walked past the living room, I could see Christmas 1989 when I had a mild junior high meltdown over a brown leather jacket. The reflection of every Fourth of July with cousins is seen in the pool on a warm summer day. Ella walking down the long hallway to her room appears like I'm walking it all over again. I could see my dad in the study, newspaper in hand, and my mom in the kitchen gazing out the window. It was almost impossible not to view the past, living in the home I grew up in. I could sing along with our theme song, quote the one-liners, find comedy in our dysfunction, name the episode, look for the life lesson, and then watch it all over again tomorrow.

Today was where I didn't want to be. Because today I cried. I cried until I got a splitting headache. Today I couldn't think straight. I couldn't even hear my own thoughts. I started at loud noises and kept getting lost in a blank stare. Today I thought I couldn't breathe. My lungs felt tight. My heart felt like it might jump out of my body. Today I didn't have the energy to get dressed, and I didn't care about taking a shower. Today there was a heavy weight pressing on my chest. Today my fingers hurt, and I wondered if there was something physically wrong with me. Could it be rheumatoid arthritis? "Maybe you are intolerant to gluten," someone suggested. Today I wondered if I would ever feel normal again. Physically. Mentally. Emotionally. Today I felt an ache up my arm, and I started shivering so badly that it turned to convulsing and I ended up in the ER. They wrote it up as anxiety. Today my stomach was nervous and nauseated and unsettled. Today I sought comfort in McDonald's french fries. I felt guilty and disgusted. Today I could only stomach toast and tea. Today I snapped at my kids and let them watch countless hours of TV. They must have wondered why I was crying all the time. Today, when I was alone, I felt like screaming at the top of my lungs, so I did. Today I felt tired—so very tired. Today I felt shame for feeling the way I do. Today I felt guilty for wasting the day and all the yesterdays, too. Today hope felt foreign, like a thing of the past. Like I lost it or it gave up on me.

"Today" was the landscape of my broken heart.

Your "today" may look different or surprisingly similar. I've come to believe that the one commonality that defines a broken heart is the *loss of hope*. What a hard thing to admit when you are a child of God.

Naming the break
is the beginning of
break/through

What happens if I admit that I feel hopeless and accept that my heart is broken?

————— ....

I was doing my best to keep it together while at lunch with my friend Rebekah. In a crowded Manhattan restaurant, we were talking a mile a minute, all at once catching up on her life in New York and trying to decide what meal to share. When it was my turn to give an update on my life, I was vague. I didn't want to be bothersome, and I didn't want my emotions to interrupt the conversation; I tried not to boil over. That's when Rebekah interrupted me and named what I couldn't. She was no stranger to the telltale signs. Rebekah was, herself, acquainted with the landscape of a broken heart. Over roast chicken and kale salad (which was likely agreed upon as a precursor to a Shake Shack burger for dinner), she called out the brokenness in me.

It was freeing. For so long, I felt like I had been locked in a room where no one could hear any cries for help. In this moment, Rebekah saw me, gaping wound and all. That day provided me permission to grieve. To let the lid off and the beans boil over. We cried and ate and talked about being broken and being whole. The conversation is one that continues between us to this day.

Naming the break is the beginning of breakthrough. Admission and acceptance of a broken heart simply mean that you are finally aware that your armor is gone. The steel has shattered; the protective layer is lost. Accepting the break is not defeat or treachery. It is not relinquishing to a life of brokenness or being bound to the thing that broke you or the very real emotions that try to choke you. Rather, it is the quiet, brave surrender to God of the hopelessness that has a hold on you. It's finally allowing Jesus and the healing power of the Cross to break through every square inch of your brokenness and pain.

This past year I began praying Psalm 139:23–24. After reading this favorite passage for the first time in in the Passion Translation, I wanted the help of the Holy Spirit to sift through *all* of *my* anxious cares. It was no longer just a prayer that David prayed. It was a prayer I knew I needed to pray too. Take a moment to pray it with me:

> God, I invite your searching gaze into my heart. Examine me through and through: find out everything that may be hidden within me. Put me to the test and sift through all my anxious cares. *See if there is any path of pain I'm walking on,* and lead me back to your glorious, everlasting ways—the path that brings me back to you. (TPT, emphasis added)

I didn't quite know what I was getting into when I began to pray that prayer, but I knew in my heart that the Lord was trying to tell me something. With sharp precision and gentle grace, He has been revealing the specific paths of pain I've been walking on. In this process of healing, things feel like they get worse before they get better. Many times it's not just about finding and understanding what broke you (the day that changed everything). It's also about what has broken you before, when you were five, ten, or fourteen and you had no language for it. When you had no skills or, perhaps, people to walk you through it. You went on. You disassociated yourself with your pain, whether you did it subconsciously as a little child or intentionally as a teen. Today, your heart broke into a million little pieces because the cracks were formed many moons ago. Your foundation was faulty, potentially for decades. While this may feel insurmountable—I felt the same way in facing my own pain—I believe the grace of God is within the crumbled foundations and among the ruins. The brokenness allows the balm of His love to flow through the places it never could before (Ps. 107:19–21 NET). It moves in and out and over and under and through all of the hurts you couldn't even name. And now it can cover them, blanket them until the heat of the Father's intense love disintegrates every last little speck of them.

ONCE YOU HAVE LIVED WITHIN THE LANDSCAPE OF A BROKEN HEART, YOU WILL THEN BE ABLE TO CALL OUT THE BREAKS IN OTHERS AS WELL AS THE BREAKTHROUGH.

Healing a broken heart is a collaboration. On our part, it takes a decision to look directly at our pain, not away from it. A willingness to let the Spirit move freely in and out of every craggy part of our hearts. Consent to get to the source of our sores and permission to find the fault that was the ticking time bomb. When we ask for healing and open our hearts to receive, God begins a work in us that He promises to bring to completion (Phil. 1:6 NIV). Because that is the way of the Cross. It is already finished. "He carried our pain, he endured punishment that made us well; because of his wounds we *have been* healed" (Isa. 53:4-5 NET). While the work is complete, the change is not always instantaneous. I wish there was a quick fix. A magic wand. A twitch of the nose. I've found it to be a journey, a redirecting from the path of pain to the path of wholeness. It's walking hand in hand with our ever-present help and allowing Him to shine a light into *all* the dark places, the rooms we have forgotten or once locked. Facing pain may be a formidable challenge, but as Henry Rollins says, "Pain is not my enemy, it is my call to greatness."[3]

Giving the Holy Spirit permission to sift through our anxious cares is the way of healing and the path to greatness. Once you have lived within the landscape of a broken heart, you will then be able to call out the breaks in others as well as the breakthrough.

The work God does in you is never just about you. It is about every person who comes after you and those walking beside you. Perhaps even for the ones who came before you.

———— ....

He gives beauty *for* ashes, Lovely Ones, the oil of joy for mourning, a garment of praise for the spirit of heaviness (Isa. 61:3). It is an exchange. We must let go of what we carry in order to receive the good gifts He would have us hold. This is the promise of being found by beauty.

Beauty is a cure for pain. It is the light that lures us to come out of hiding, that brings color to everything—our todays, tomorrows, and even yesterdays. Beauty longs to radiate its incandescent hues over the landscape of our hearts, transforming us from the dull, faded carbon copies of creation that we have become, returning us to the masterpieces that we were made to be—reflecting His beauty—to be the very God-colors of the earth (Matt. 5:14–16 MSG).

the liv
& livin

CHAPTER FOUR | THE LIVED-IN AND LIVING HOME

d-in
g home

FOUR

"Imagine yourself as a living house. God comes in to rebuild that house. He is building quite a different house from the one you thought of—throwing out a new wing here, putting on an extra floor there, running up towers, making courtyards. You thought you were being made into a decent little cottage: but He is building a palace. He intends to come and live in it Himself."

—C. S. LEWIS, *MERE CHRISTIANITY*[1]

The first time I walked into our house, there was so much blue. Blue-patterned wallpaper from the moment you stepped through the front door, to the right and to the left, and all along the hallway. Straight ahead, a large sunken living room with French doors dressed in blue drapes that looked out on a kidney bean–shaped pool. Around the corner, a dining room wrapped in ice blue–flocked fleur-de-lis wallpaper—fuzzy to the touch. And at one end of the hall, a kitchen donned in two hues of blue shag carpet and Dutch Delft blue flowers crawling up the walls, crowned with a border of blue Japanese pagodas that quite possibly housed little blue-painted people. I only wish I would've looked a little closer. I didn't think much of the excess of blue because the year was 1986 and I was nine.

Today, it's 2017, and I am thirty-nine. Thirty years later and I am living in the same house, on the same street. The blue sailed away in the late '90s only to be replaced by brown, and for the past eleven years, the house has been in a slow metamorphosis from brown to beige to white.

I never imagined, in a million years, that I'd be living in my childhood home as an adult. That, somehow, the beloved place where I grew would be the same place my children would grow, too. It's as strange and magical as you might imagine. It's healing and sometimes haunting. It's both comfortable and confining. The best way I can describe it to you is that the house feels like a person, a protective old friend. A kind, watchful grandpa who holds your heritage, your stories, your heart.

Here I am, thirty years, one husband, four kids, two dogs, and one cat later. Back in my childhood home for eleven years now. And for these past eleven years, I've been slowly trying to make the house my own. We've switched out the shag carpet for wood floors, repurposed rooms, and painted spaces. In our master bedroom we've put in large wood-plank flooring that we painted white, changed the dark dining room into a bright playroom, and hung a swing and disco ball in our living room (some of these changes making my parents scratch their heads).

Decorating. Redecorating. Remodeling. I've seen it all over the years in the grandpa-person-of-a-house. During my senior year of high school, my parents remodeled the blue pagoda kitchen and added a master suite and home office. We lived in a construction zone. Clear plastic tarps divided the house from what it was to what it would be. Part old, part new, joined as one to grow old together. The blue drifted away as a forest of greens and mauvy pinks settled in. Viny flowers and ivy now patterned our lives.

I've watched the house take on different shapes and wear countless coats of color and patterns over the years. Its walls have held photographs and memories, secrets and stories. It has withstood the weight of my family's world in good times and bad. It has taken in many precious people, some of whom I can now visit only by memory. This house always welcomed change and allowed for more room.

———— ....

I believe God speaks to us in the language we know best. Yes, always through and confirmed by Scripture, but many times His whispers come by way of surroundings that are familiar and through people who are trusted. Music. Words. Art. Allegory. Imagery. And always through nature—His art—the art every artist imitates.

I'm a house girl, a homebody, a nester, which felt problematic when my seemingly solid definition of home completely unraveled. I've never wanted to go far from home. As far back as I can remember, I've been attached to the homes I've lived in, to the feeling of being home. Yet only within the unraveling did I discover that I was knit with a heart that beats home. At the intersection of these conflictions, I came full circle to a Sunday school saying that I heard growing up: "Jesus makes His home in your heart." In my brokenness, I began to wonder, *Is this just a childhood cliché of the churched?*

It wasn't that I was questioning my faith. It was more that I was deeply confused at how Jesus could make His home in my mangled mess of a heart. If I believe that Jesus *is* love, freedom, and healing and that He is in me, then my life should reflect that. Yet, when my world crumbled and I, at last, was able to relent and accept the state of my heart being broken, the door flung wide open, and things began to bubble up and out of my heart. Ugly things. Things I didn't think were in me because they had never been revealed or were only ever faintly felt. Things like anger, jealousy, bitterness, and unforgiveness.

Jesus lived among that?

Yes. He was right in the middle of it.

For six years home was the painful fixture in front of me, behind me, and within me. It looked like a demolition of my definition, a realization of a false security, and a flattening of my foundation, followed by slow construction of the true definition and a firm foundation. It's clever and now so clear that *home* would be the language our Father would use to help me better understand.

Although home was a place I often wanted to run from, it would also be the very language that God in His kindness would draw me back with.

———— ....

The heart is a home.

You and me, a living home.

Imperfect people abiding with perfection.

Humans holding heaven within.

Beauty living within the broken.

It is the narrative of the centuries, broken people searching for God, who is, all along, at home within. Ephesians 3:17 says, "May Christ through your faith *actually* dwell, settle down—abide—make his permanent home in your hearts. May you be rooted deep in love and founded securely on love" (AMPC, emphasis added).

Within my broken, jagged heart, Jesus is at home. Within your broken, jagged heart, Jesus is at home. This is beauty within the broken—Christ *in* us.

Trusting Him as Lord and Savior, receiving Him, is the key to opening the lock on the home of your heart. And as you become more at home with this revelation, your roots will grow deep into God's love, and you will be made strong.

You will be made *strong*.

The heart will not stay broken.

And you will not remain its prisoner.

His Kingdom will come—within.

And His beauty will cure the broken.

I wonder what broke your heart.

What faulty place or thing holds your security?

I'm no longer running from home, and I'm letting the One in residence work *within* me. The builder is clearing out debris and smoothing rough edges. He is laying a new foundation. He is sanding and staining and constructing. This is the way a home is built. With strategy and planning. He always executes with precision. And it takes *time*. Time and work. God is not into turnkey homes; we are all custom-built. And this architect, this builder, does not cut corners!

When our kitchen was taped off with plastic tarps, it felt like we were living in a construction zone. It was the dead of winter in the Midwest, and it was cold. The house felt broken in half. The kitchen didn't function at full capacity. The new addition was difficult to live in because it was in progress. We had to adjust and make the best of it.

But when at last the addition was complete, it made the home more livable and enjoyable. There was room for more. More life. More living. I'm finding that in our living homes, it is the same. God is always making room for more. More of Him. More life.

Just as we long to express ourselves within our lived-in

home through paint colors, furniture, and art, God is longing to express Himself in the interiors of our hearts. And when we allow the truth that Jesus makes a home—takes up residence—in our hearts to really sink in, it's nothing short of revolutionary.

Whether you are going through a complete renovation or a simple update, Jesus is right there, living in it with you. He's there holding up the tarp, sitting on the old side with you as you adjust to living "under construction." He's also on the other side, building a new foundation and making room for more. Change, even for the better, is painful and full of hard work. But when the refresh, the remodeling, the decorating is complete, what a lovely, spacious home you will have with a strong, solid foundation, sure to withstand any storm.

The following are a few photos of my home. I look at these images now, and I see more than a pretty space. I see the slow process of change over eleven years. I see what the rooms looked like in years past. I see the detail, work, and effort that went into the changes. But now, mostly, I see a reflection of the remodel of my heart; a living home that could have shrunk but has only enlarged and is getting stronger by the day.

look for
lovely

CHAPTER FIVE | LOOK FOR A LOVELY THING

FIVE

A thing of beauty is a joy for ever:
Its loveliness increases; it will never
Pass into nothingness

—JOHN KEATS

It could have been the air rolling off the Santa Catalina Mountains outside my parents' home in Tucson or the pink Southwest sunset creating a shadow behind a saguaro cactus. Maybe it was the long, lazy days I filled lying by the pool or time spent scoping out new shops. Perhaps it was playing with my children and relaxing with my family (before it was broken) in the summery sun in February (heaven on earth for a Midwesterner). Maybe it was all of the Mexican food. Whatever it was, something lovely was swinging below the desert stars.

One afternoon, I exchanged the lounge chair for the leather

sectional. I curled up on the sofa—just me and a magazine (you understand the rare indulgence if you are a mother). There I was thumbing through *Domino,* getting a closer look at designs that inspired and reading articles on new and interesting trends when I came across a short feature on a blog called "Absolutely Beautiful Things." I grabbed my laptop to investigate further, and like that, I was hooked. It was the first blog I remember visiting.

I found beauty. Or did beauty find me? Either way it was online and unexpected. Here I was with the Sonoran Desert out my window, and I was discovering pretty in pixels and inspiration from the web.

I have *Domino* to thank for introducing me to blogs and Anna Spiro of Absolutely Beautiful Things to thank for an introduction to beauty-gone-digital.

My last few days lounging left me thinking about this thing called a blog. *Are there a lot of blogs? Do you need experience? Can I write about whatever I want to? Should I do this? I need a name. Who would make me a logo? How does one start a blog?*

I didn't have the answers, but I decided I was going to do it. I was going to start a blog. I would get myself an online address and create an online home where I could invite others over and share. I would now have a place to write besides my journals, a place to collect inspiration other than manila folders in a drawer, a place to share with anyone and everyone who was looking for lovely.

In those days, I often got texts from friends asking, "Do you have any gift ideas for my mother-in-law?" "Where should I eat in Chicago?" "What is your favorite brand for this and that and those?" Now I could answer, not just with a *Send* but with a *Publish*.

From time to time, I am asked where I came up with the name La La Lovely. It just kind of came to me, sitting on the sectional in Tucson. I wrote it down with a Sharpie on a mini notepad piece of paper and tucked it in my Bible, where it is still tucked between Acts 1 and 2 to this day. I always loved the word "lovely"; it may be my favorite adjective. And after a recent ten-year anniversary trip to Paris and as a momentary Rosetta Stone French student, I seemed to have a thing for "la." I liked the look of it and the sound of it. "La La" sounded light, fun, and carefree. It was catchy, and it caught me. I've found that, like any name, it becomes you. La La is what all my boys have called their older sister, Ella. Nothing to do with the blog, of course, everything to do with how they could pronounce "Ella" at the age of one and two. La La seemed to be our tune.

I left Tucson with a sunburn and a name.

I returned home to the unrelenting Chicago cold to unpack suitcases and secure a URL.

A friend created a logo for my new blog, which included a bird on a chandelier.

And one month later, late at night, sitting crisscross-applesauce on my big brown couch, I took a try at my first post. It began with a Sara Teasdale quote "Look for a lovely thing and you will find it." And I went on to say...

Lovely things…we all come across them in our everyday lives whether aware of it or not. Sometimes we seek out, with great determination, very special things and sometimes our minds are so occupied and our steps are so hurried that we rush right past them without a thought. Sometimes, best of all, when we keep our eyes wide open with wonder we just happen upon them…little lovely gifts that are just set out before us.

It was never just about finding things. It was about looking for the lovely. Noticing what gifts were already given.

Noticing is the art.

———— ....

A few years ago, I had the word "Flânerie" washi-taped over my bed.

Odd, I know, to have a word that means "the act of strolling" hanging in hot pink over your bed.[1] But when I sank into my sheets, I wanted this word to sink into me.

The term "flânerie" came about sometime in the sixteenth or seventeenth century; it can best be defined as walking slowly without a hurry, sauntering, or idling and could often be pegged as wasting time.

Of course, the flâneur didn't see it as a waste of time. They wandered the streets looking for curiosities, an urban explorer of sorts. The looking must have been just as important as the finding because I read somewhere that in the 1800s it became fashionable to walk a pet turtle to set a slower pace. People in Paris were walking turtles to slow down—to slow down enough to notice the things around them.

Eventually what was once defined as a waste of time was redefined by authors like Sainte-Beuve, who said, "To flâne is the very opposite of doing nothing." And Honoré de Balzac, who described flânerie as "the gastronomy of the eye."[2]

What we notice, the curiosities we find, can redefine what we or others have labeled a waste.

I've found that it's easy to notice, to be a flâneur, when you are visiting a new city or even an eclectic store. It's not difficult to let your eyes wander slowly over the carefully curated bookshelves at your friend's new house. But to notice beauty, to look for a lovely thing and find it in your own home, that is an entirely different thing. To walk the turtle down the hall past three messy bedrooms and straight into yours with all of its memories of sleepless nights. But over there on the nightstand is the picture of you and yours. And before there were difficult times, there was only love. There is still love. It just takes the art of noticing to see it.

Finding beauty in the brokenness sometimes requires looking back. Not getting lost in the past or living there but rather finding the beauty that was there and giving thanks for it.

In front of my desk I have a photo of a cactus. I love the Southwest. I have since I was a girl. It's beauty to me. But some days when I look up at the sage-colored cactus I feel a tinge of pain. Like when a song comes on the radio and it reminds you of a time, of a someone who is no longer with you. Of love. And of loss. It's our nature to avoid pain. To push it aside. I have so many good memories. But the fact is, after the divorce, Tucson will never again be what it was, what I always thought it would be—the place we would return to again and again to all be together. Now it's like a stain on my heart. My memory gone musty. The cactus rotting.

In my flânerie of the memory, I notice this about myself: I let the "what is" soil the "what was." The pain in today mocks what was and muddies the memory of it.

During my parents' lengthy divorce process, we had two medical crises in our family. After both instances, my family gathered at my house, the family home. The first time, my dad was sitting on the sofa, eating takeout from his favorite Japanese restaurant, watching TV. My mom was cleaning up in the kitchen, and my brother and I were sitting on the steps that join the kitchen to the sunken family room. We sat between the two—the two rooms and parents. For a moment, everything felt as it should, as I wanted it to. It didn't last long, but I held on to the evanescent moment with a clawing grip until it slipped through my fingers and reality smacked me in the face. I grieved.

The second time, almost exactly a year later, I was ill with acute liver injury. It was very scary, and in an instant life became very clear. All that mattered was people. Again, everyone gathered at my house, the family home. My husband and children were at my side, and so were my mom and my dad. This time I sat on the sofa, in the same spot my dad had sat. My mom and kids on the step. My dad standing in the kitchen. For a moment everything felt as it should. It didn't last long, but once again I held on to the evanescent moment with a clawing grip until it slipped through my fingers and reality smacked me in the face. And I grieved. Only this time, I also gave thanks. Maybe it was the sickness? Maybe it was that more time had passed? Most likely it was because God was mending my heart. I gave thanks for "what was." For the memories that were good. For the love I felt growing up. For the cherished moments of magic in my childhood. For the care. For the support. For the family that was. For the family that is. "What is" could not sully "what was."

I was walking nowhere, confined to the couch, and I was a flâneur. Wandering the streets of my memory and exploring the good to be grateful for.

Psalm 34:12 says, "Who out there has a lust for life, can't wait each day to come upon beauty?" (MSG). The way to get back to the lust for life is through beauty. Even the expectation of it. Sometimes beauty is best seen with our eyes closed or when we walk the pace of a turtle.

My Lovely Things List

today I noticed ...

CHAPTER SIX | A LETTER TO MY LITTLES

Dear one,

Life is hard, dear one. I want to say with all my heart that it is easy — that it is beautiful and breezy — but it is not. At least, not all of the time. I should be clear on that. I wouldn't have believed it if my parents had told me. But I am telling you.

Know that there are moments of utter bliss and moments of pure anguish. Moments when you feel your heart might burst out of an overload of love and all things good and hopeful. And then there are moments when you feel your heart might break in half. Maybe not just break in half, but shatter into a thousand tiny pieces. Pieces you are convinced can never be put together again.

But these are, may I remind you, moments. And there is much life to be lived in between the highest of highs and lowest of lows. The in-betweens are the everydays—the days you decide to live the best that you possibly can, even if that simply means putting one foot in front of the other, peering through shattered rose-colored glasses.

Dearest, you must learn to keep in step on both the rocky terrain and the lush green pastures of life. You will be fooled to believe there is great scarcity in goodness when life has turned sour, just as you will be deceived to not take notice of it when life is overflowing with sweetness. Do not be so accustomed to your state, whether high or low, that you cannot find beauty in a moment. For in a moment, anything and everything can change. The taste from bitter to sweet. The dance from fast to slow.

In a moment, the wind can change, and so can the season. The long-awaited warmth of spring still brings rain, and the bitter-cold winter has its warmth.

On a neighborhood sidewalk, note the daisy growing between two rocks. Pick it and put it in your pocket, behind your loved one's ear, or between the pages of a book. When you find yourself wandering the stony trails of life, notice the daisy pushing up from between the gravel, and don't be startled when the aroma of the daisy you put in your pocket, long ago, fills the air.

And as you peel each petal away from its sunshine center and your mind tells you, "He loves you not." I can assure your heart that it always ends with "HE LOVES YOU!"

And because of that heavenly healing love, the thousand tiny pieces of your heart can be put together again.

This is living—highs, lows, nothing, bliss, heartbreak, everything. Days of darkness and sometimes nights filled with light.

And although it is hard—sometimes physically painful—you live it and you feel it. Because if you can feel the hard times, you can feel the goodness of better days. And feeling it all is living it all, and living it all is in fact life. Crazy, beautiful, messed-up, brutal, and bright life.

Live it. Live it well. Live it the best
you possibly can ... and you will
be a happy soul.

XO

a chan
scener

CHAPTER SEVEN | A CHANGE OF SCENERY

SEVEN

"Getting found almost always means being lost for a while."

—ANNE LAMOTT, *SMALL VICTORIES*[1]

I tried running away a number of times as a kid.

"I'm running away!" I barked before turning my nose up in the air and shuffling down the long hallway to my room. I can't be certain if I was in trouble, mad, or unhappy. "Here is a suitcase," my mom quickly retorted. I was young enough that she called my bluff. I crawled out the window anyways, just to see what it felt like, not leaving through the door. Another, more memorable time that I ran away was in junior high. While my parents were a few houses down playing tennis in the street, I had the brilliant idea to drive my dad's car around the driveway. In the process of backing the car out of the garage, I swiped my mom's blue minivan and gave it a decorative maroon stripe down the side. Instead of confessing, I ran away to the park where I conceded to live under the slide, surviving on snacks that my cousin, Kristin, would bring me. I rode my bike back home by dusk and divulged. The truth was I was more afraid of my face being on a milk carton than I was of facing my parents.

Running away for me has always been a go-to when life gets to be too much. I didn't lose this penchant to run when I turned twenty-one. It's been an interesting and sobering lesson to learn that many times we carry our childhood responses with us into adulthood. Yet I sometimes wonder if we are wired to want to run away from home, from problems, from difficult situations. I imagine this goes back to the garden—Adam and Eve wanting to hide and God banishing them from the garden, their home.

Two years into my family unraveling, into my unraveling, I found that I spent a large portion of my time daydreaming about running away. I felt that God had run from *me*. This wasn't true, but my feelings deceived me.

Every night I could be found standing at the kitchen sink, scrubbing and sudsing pots and pans. And there I'd ponder where I'd go. England? *Predictable, that is the first place anyone would look for me.* France? *The language barrier sounds appealing.* I'd travel in my mind. I'd lose myself. I'd even tell those close to me I just might jump on a plane and go—O'Hare to anywhere. I wondered if they believed me or if I even believed myself. It turns out that I'd always lose my gumption, just like when I was a girl. My imagination, although vivid and lively, always lost to its much stronger opponent: responsibility. Responsibility always wins with me. And, in the end, responsibility was the thing that kept reminding me that four little lives depend upon me. Even if I was to run away just for a little while, to them it might as well be forever. Because they would always remember that time their mom ran away. Left. Disappeared, even if only for days. And, knowing what I know now, it might have affected them for some kind of ever. I traveled back and forth many times in my mind, but I stayed put in my broken American dream. That is, until I found myself, ticket in hand, on my way to London, searching for something I didn't realize I already possessed.

Over dinner, my lifelong friends shared that their family was heading to London in a few weeks. I'm not sure if they saw my face wrinkle, if they felt bad for me, if I jokingly invited myself, or if they said, "You should come!" In any case, it was a definite possibility.

YOU MUST GET LOST BEFORE
YOU CAN BE FOUND.

I was grateful for the option, but I talked myself out of it about twenty-two times. I said yes. I said no. I said, "I don't know." My sister said if I went, I could live off the trip for at least six months. "Go, and take courage," she said. I said no. And then I gave a final yes and white-knuckled the arm-rest the entire eight hours over the ocean.

I walked around the city with my friends, went in and out

of shops, ate fish and chips, drank tea, and opened my eyes to behold the breathtaking and elaborate architecture. We toured Winston Churchill's bunker, and I tried to trace his courage and wrap my head around his resolve. I ate caviar-covered sushi at Harrods and attended Hillsong's Colour Conference; I knew God was there. I cracked open the door to my living home; I opened my heart.

We took the Tube back to our hotel at Piccadilly Circus. Lights shone brightly, and my heart began to let the light in. I said goodnight to my friends and wandered around the city to find dinner. The only place open was McDonald's. In my hotel room, I let out a loud laugh at the thought of caviar-covered sushi for lunch and McDonald's for dinner. I felt a chill at the thought of the never-ending winter and my longing to get lost in a town like London. And as I gave thanks for my french fries, I felt I was being found. *Thank you for finding me in London.* And with the bite of my Big Mac came a whisper: *I didn't have to find you. I've been with you all along.*

I cried and shoved the rest of the salty fries down, laughing at the beautiful, desperate, hopeful, and very personal hotel room scene. There I was in my favorite foreign city, a city I loved before I ever visited it, eating American fast food from the place my mom took us to on our worst days. But the beauty is, that's me: a complicated American who grew up eating McDonald's for comfort. And He met me, loved me, in my most personal, complicated way.

That night before bed, I thought about feeling lost, feeling found, being at home, and running away from home. I thought about how I wasn't really *found*; I just recognized

what I'd received all along and rejected the lie I had believed: *all alone.*

You must get lost before you can be found.

Two days later, I was en route to Durrington-on-Sea. This train ride had always been a part of my daydream. It was what I'd visualize as I scrubbed and sudsed and stared out the window I'd been looking out my entire life. I'd picture: me, earphones, the music from *Amélie*, pens, paper, a crazy-cool European design magazine, courage in my heart, and a twinkle in my eye. I was finally on my adventure, traveling solo in Europe by train, in my beloved England, to visit my dear friend Maggie. I felt like the bee's knees. Like ten-year-old me, freshly freckled, riding my bike to Edgebrook on my own for the very first time. It was a taste of wild freedom that I hadn't known for so long. This daydreaming romantic was living outside of her mind and on the very pages of her life.

I think of Adam, of Eve, hiding. And I wonder if what they truly wanted, behind all their coverings, was to be found, seen, accepted in their nakedness, *at their worst.*

I thought I wanted to run, but what I really wanted, what I've always wanted, was to be found.

And I was. I was found in the truth that I am never alone, even in my hotel room while eating a Big Mac. I was found in friendship that made room for one more traveler. I was found on a train ride from daydream to London to Worthing. I was found in toast and tea and talking into the night with my British bestie. I was found in a small English church

on the last day of my trip, where the pastor spoke the same words my sister gave me at the start, "Take courage."

I opened my hands to the offering. I took what the change of scenery offered. I took what God had been waiting for me to receive. I took *courage*.

En route to healing and wholeness I've been taking trips. Not all have been as elaborate as the trip to England. All, however, were detours that shook up my everyday. If there was an offer, I took it. Sometimes it looked like sharing a room with my friend's three children in a small New York City bedroom. Other times it looked like a road trip to my in-laws in Atlanta, a bloggers' conference I had already attended the year before, or Tucson with friends, keeping a fifteen-year tradition, facing the trusty mountains out the windows and the memories within. Some days it was as close as a short drive to the apple orchard.

I THOUGHT I WANTED TO RUN, BUT WHAT I REALLY WANTED, WHAT I'VE ALWAYS WANTED, WAS TO BE FOUND.

These days I like to think I've outgrown my urge to run away. I've learned, instead, to make room for getaways because getting away from trials and having a change of scenery helps us not to lose ourselves during hard times. It helps you to see beyond the problem right in front of you, to think within a bigger picture, to see life in its fullness, and to feel found.

A change of scenery is not just a good idea; it is necessary and essential. This is an offering from Him to me and me to you. Get away and take courage! "He reached down from heaven and took me out of my greatest trials. He rescued me from deep waters" (Ps. 18:16 TLB).

01 / To where does your soul feel connected—even if you have never been?

02 / For what kind of getaway does your heart yearn?

03 / How can you "take courage" today?

04 / How has God "found" you this week?

EIGHT

*"It is the custom of every good mother after her children are
asleep to rummage in their minds and put things straight for next
morning, repacking into their proper places the many articles that
have wandered during the day. When you wake in the morning,
the naughtinesses and evil passions with which you went to bed
have been folded up small and placed at the bottom of your
mind; and on the top, beautifully aired, are spread out prettier
thoughts, ready for you to put on."*

—J. M. BARRIE, *PETER PAN*[1]

You've heard of pregnancy brain, mom brain, and brain fog. Now, may I introduce you to mental clutter.

I live a lot of my life in my head. My inner monologue is chatty. I make up scenarios. I replay the day. I calculate. I have conversations. I hear the tune of background music in my brain. Personality tests have confirmed what I've always suspected—that my inner life is busier than most. I believe it, but I also have a hunch that I'm not the only one plagued with wandering worries and mental clutter that stacks up like clothes on the closet floor.

mental clutter

noun, see also (similar), physical clutter.

1. The background thoughts that pile up and clog up the mind
2. The white noise of your soul
3. The soundtrack of your brokenness
4. The stories we tell ourselves

Personally, I don't subscribe to pregnancy brain. I mean, I do because it is real and it happens. But it never goes away. It just gets a name change: mom brain. At this stage, I'm left to wonder if mom brain will ever go away. I have my doubts as being a mom lasts a lifetime, and I suspect that just about the time mom brain goes into remission, it has a high probability of morphing into menopausal brain.

All of this lady brain business was operating at high levels when the divorce dropped like a bomb. Consequently, it was the same time I was pregnant with my fourth and had just finished nursing my nine-month-old, Liam Brave. By the time Rocco was born, the mental clutter was, shall we say, of hoarder proportions.

There was lack of sleep, a new baby, an eighteen-month-old, two elementary school–age children, a husband trying to build a business, and the heartache of my family falling apart. The fog was so dense I was drowning in it like the Golden Gate Bridge.

I tried to navigate through the brain fog. I thought maybe shifting my focus from the fog to smaller, achievable tasks would help clear my mind. So, I gave myself a list of to-dos—a list that was almost always unfeasible to accomplish from the brain reserve I was living off of. I made it a never-ending pursuit to see how high I could climb above the cloud that was suffocating me. I wanted to prove to myself (and everyone else) that I could function in low visibility. Yet what I thought would distract me and help me to rise above only brought more clutter. The list, the expectations, became like microwave popcorn of the brain. *Do this.* Pop. *Do that.* Pop. *Don't forget this.* Pop. *You forgot that.* Pop. Pop. Pop. I couldn't focus on any task long enough to check it off my lofty list.

The noise got louder, the clutter climbed higher, the fog became more dense.

I began to wonder if I could disconnect from my own brain. *If physical clutter can be cleaned up one cabinet, one drawer at a time, is mental clutter cleaned up the same way—one thought at a time?*

Wouldn't a purge be better? A Dumpster in front of the house like you see on an episode of *Hoarders*. Taking an entire Saturday to get rid of anything that I don't find to be useful or beautiful. Eliminating anything and everything that doesn't bring me happiness in the Marie Kondo way: all at once, all at once.

But our minds have more cabinets, drawers, knickknacks, books, framed memories, trophies, souvenirs, trinkets, and cobwebs than any brick-and-mortar home could ever hold.

Maybe this requires more than a purge? Sorting. Filing. Discarding. Give away. Keep. Donate. No, it was a deep cleaning that was needed. A good scrub. A lot of suds. As dishes must be washed, so must our minds.

The way to declutter the mind is with the washing of the Word (Eph.5:26 AMP).

It starts with being honest about the mess and laying your burden down at His feet. It begins with believing the Son is still there, not above it all but beside you in the dense haze, waiting for you to receive the heat of His love that will burn the fog from the foreground of your mind.

I've found that when I allow this light in, the radiance of God's love evaporates the encroaching air, and I'm left with what is *really* there. I'm face-to-face with the cabinets, drawers, memories—everything I've kept, all that I've held on to.

I'm left with the lies I've told myself.

I told myself that nothing would ever be the same again. I told myself I wouldn't be taken care of, that I would lack. I told myself that I was a bad mother because I snapped often. I told myself I was a bad wife because I couldn't meet every expectation—I am not domestic enough, am not supportive enough, don't cook with organic ingredients enough. I told myself I was a bad daughter because I couldn't keep everyone and everything together. I told myself I was a bad blogger because I wasn't bringing in enough numbers, views, or dollars. I told myself I was a bad friend because a few old friendships had fizzled. I told myself I was a bad Christian because I didn't do enough for God. I told myself I must be out of God's will. The story I tell myself is that I am not good *enough*, again and again and again.

When the fog lifts, we are left with the opinions we've packed away, whether they are others' or our own. "You haven't been a good friend to me. You are a lousy daughter. You're the worst mom ever." We've heard things like this in heated moments and honest conversations. Whether they were meant literally or figuratively, these words spoken cause mental clutter.

We have to be honest with what we find, with what is right in front of us. We have to come clean with ourselves and God about hoarding what He has asked us not to carry. We have to tell ourselves the truth about what we have held on to—the hurt and pain packed away with our own hands, as if they were precious heirlooms. These are not things we want our children or their children to inherit. But if we don't clear them out and deal with them, then they will become a hand-me-down, passed down to our children, who will be left to unclutter our messes as well as their own.

Are there stories you need to untell yourself, too? Lies you've agreed with along the way?

This is how we do it, how we untell the tale and redirect the trajectory.

We filter it through truth.

Just as we filter our possessions through the sift of "Is it beautiful?" "Does this serve a purpose?" "Does it make me happy?" we must filter our thoughts through a sieve of "Is it

authentic, real, honorable, admirable, beautiful, respectful, pure, holy, merciful, and kind?" (Phil. 4:8 TPT).

Philippians (4:6–8 TPT, emphasis added) says, "Don't be pulled in different directions or worried about *a thing*. Be saturated in prayer throughout *each day*, offering your faith-filled requests before God with overflowing gratitude. *Tell him every detail of your life*, then God's wonderful peace that transcends human understanding will make the answers known to you through Jesus Christ."

This is my sponge, my soap, my cleansing water.

———— ....

Today, as I write about mental clutter, I'm lost in the fog myself, and it's not lost on me that, of course, it is happening this way. I'm weighed down by the heavy air I want to see others freed from. I'm truly learning to face what's in front of me, but now I'm left with some big subconscious stressors in my life. It's 11 a.m., and I'm in my pajamas and have decided to lie back down because I can't quite figure out where to start. *I should be writing.* Pop. *But the kids are off school.* Pop. *I should be playing games or coming up with some craft activity, like all the good moms do.* Pop. Pop.

What if this or that happens? Pop. *How am I going to meet my deadline?* Pop. Pop. *What if the doctor finds something other than anxiety?* Pop. *How will I ever handle more change that is coming?* Pop. Pop. Pop.

Get dressed? Pray? Write? Walk? Sometimes the smallest decision feels like the biggest. All I know is that I need to move. I've found that walking is a silent command of the body to the mind—*I'm moving now, you be still.* Emily Dickinson said so well, "If your nerve deny you—Go above your nerve."[2] I take all that is making me nervous to the One above all.

———— ....

What if this or that happens?

"Now to Him who is able to [carry out His purpose and] do superabundantly more than all that we dare ask or think [infinitely beyond our greatest prayers, hopes, or dreams], according to His power that is at work within us" (Eph. 3:20 AMP).

How am I going to meet my deadline?

"I've picked you. I haven't dropped you. Don't panic. I'm with you. There's no need to fear for I'm your God. I'll give you strength. *I'll help you.* I'll hold you steady, keep a firm grip on you" (Isa. 41:10 MSG, emphasis mine).

What if the doctor finds something other than anxiety?

"I am the LORD who heals you" (Exod. 15:26 NIV).

How will I ever handle more change that is coming?

"I (Jesus Christ) am the same yesterday and today and forever" (Heb. 13:8 NIV).

I find myself in His story. This beauty is offered every day.

I put on my yoga pants and a little mascara and head downstairs. On the treadmill, I remind myself, yet again, that as I do the dishes daily, I must tend to the mental clutter every day or my thinking will get as crusty as last night's lasagna pan.

CHAPTER NINE | CLEARING THE CACHE

NINE

"What cannot be said will be wept."

—SAPPHO[1]

This morning I snuck into Ella's school chapel service. It was a little strange. For one, my fourteen-year-old daughter was leading worship— not just singing in the background, but leading her entire junior high school. Leading me. How could this be my baby girl? Also strange because it is the school I attended at her age. And the guest speaker just happened to be my former high school pastor. With Ella singing and Mike speaking, you couldn't have paid me to miss it.

My husband, Stephen, my mom, my sister-in-law, Lindsay, and my niece Hopie came along too (Ella had a fan club).

We chose seats a good distance from the students, as any wise middle-school parent would do. And before I could even get my coat off, I found myself carried away in the music, watching my daughter lead worship so freely, as if this was simply what she was born to do. I wish I could have bottled up the moment, that feeling, it was that special.

Just at the point when I was beginning to have major déjà vu, Mike got up to speak; only he sat. He sat down with a group of students huddled around the platform and began to talk to them about their value. He then asked one of the sixth-grade girls to stand up. I sat back in equal parts ease and long-lost familiarity, and I teared up in the tender moment. He shared what he saw in her, the ways God would use her, and over and over her *worth*—not determined by her peers, not even determined by her parents, but determined by God, who says she is fearfully and wonderfully made. I began to cry, not dainty tears that sneak out the corners of your eyes and can be blotted away without collateral damage to your mascara. No, my tears obliterated all evidence that I put makeup on in the first place. I didn't have words to explain this wave of emotion to my concerned husband or mother or not even myself—except to say that I *was* that girl. I was that young girl, uncertain of herself, of her value, of her place, of her purpose. I was the young girl that Mike spoke to more than twenty-five years ago, in that same space, in the same fatherly fashion. In some form of emotional time travel, I could feel what I felt all those years ago: how badly I wanted to matter and how desperately I wanted someone to believe in me. And not just believe in what I could do, but believe in who I was.

After he finished encouraging the young one, he asked

for another student to pray for her. I remembered those moments too—awkward, sweaty palms, heart beating fast—thinking to myself, *Will someone stand up? Should I? I should. I will.*

I was given opportunity to *do*. This is where and how I learned to pray and to lead—not by osmosis but by taking the opportunity to try, to fail, to fall, to get back up, and to try again. It's not often one's present is refreshed by a tangible flashback.

It was like clearing my cache, deleting the cookies.

———— ....

I'm not great with change. There are things I always want to change, like my hair, my weight, my kitchen. There are things I think about changing, like where I live. And then there are a handful of things I believed would never, should never change; things I never considered could change. You know, the things that never cross your mind as a possibility. You have those things too, don't you? I've found that when the "should nevers" change, suddenly everything is a possibility for change. And "what if" becomes the recurring start of the scenarios I tell myself. The truth is, the older I get, the more I realize and am trying to accept that nothing stays the same. Seed to flower. Child to adult. Young to old. Life to death. Death to Life.

In a world of change, "a Father of lights, with whom there is no variation or the slightest hint of change" (James 1:17 NET) becomes the most refreshing truth there is. Christ offers us a security that no person ever can.

I think the reason why my eyes were red and glassy today, why the second application of mascara didn't quite cut it and the concealer couldn't conceal it, is that I felt something so familiar. For a brief moment, the thousand little and big changes between the 1990s and now didn't exist. It was me and the one thing that has remained the same through it all—a God who will always be saying, "You matter, Trina. I believe in you, Trina. You are fearfully and wonderfully made, designed for a purpose."

The history was still there.

———— ....

I believe in the power of a good refresh. From the inside out. From the outside in. I don't discount the kind that often gets overlooked yet helps us to see things in a different way: a fresh coat of paint, a new patterned pillow, pink-polished nails, a new haircut. Even outward updates can help us to see things in a new light, like lenses giving tired eyes a clear vision of beauty that was blurred. These welcome changes don't solve the unwelcome ones we'd wish away; rather, they bring out a quality in what we already have, in who we already are.

If getting a gel manicure puts pep in your step, shellac those nails in OPI's "A Great Opera-tunity." If having fresh flowers in your home adds life and color, add flowers in your shopping cart at the grocery store. If your walls look tired (or scary like my boy's bathroom walls do), give them a fresh coat of paint; change the color if you like, or maybe keep it the same hue. If you've been eyeing that pink shaggy pillow for years on the interwebs and walked past the discount version at Target this past week, pick it up. It's not impulsive if you've known it would sweeten up your bedroom for the past twenty-four months. Try that pixie cut or that new color; hair grows back, and color can be corrected. Personally, I go for Dior Show mascara, the one that smells like roses. It opens up my eyes, and when I cry it all off, my soul is opened.

I wonder what kind of refresh you need.

If you need color or a good cry.

Is your view, your browsing, obstructed by the years of cookies and cache stored in the deep history of your heart?

Does your history need clearing, or do you need to return to it to bookmark the beauty God called out in you so long ago?

Lovely One, Jesus has been "refreshing tired bodies; and restoring tired souls" (Jer. 31:25 MSG) for a very long time. Refresh and restore. It's as if He is restoring us back to our factory settings. Back to the way we were originally made. Back to the purpose we were designed for. And anything that gets in the way of our initial design sooner or later must be refreshed and restored.

———— ....

It was a strange thing, crying like I did today. It was overwhelming, emptying, and freeing. Sometimes there are things so deep within us that we can no longer name them; we just have to let them out and let go. Let go of all of the "should nevers" and years of "what ifs." All I know is that I let that little girl in me accept the beauty she couldn't fully receive all those years ago. The cache was cleared. I took what I needed and reapplied my mascara.

CLEARING THE CACHE | 125

disconr
connec

TEN

"What the soul hardly realizes is that, unbeliever or not, his loneliness is really a homesickness for God."

—DOM HUBERT VAN ZELLER, *WE DIE STANDING UP*[1]

I've noticed that I've developed this habit when I'm feeling a little less than. Less than myself. Less than a wife. Less than a mom. Less than a daughter. Less than a friend. Less than connected, maybe?

I log on to feel connected.

I sign on to hang out.

With the swipe of a screen, I think, *I will find something.* And I do. Recipes, quotes, and my childhood friend's cute kid, dressed in festive Christmas jammies. But there are many more *somethings* I see. Things I'm missing, according to my Instagram feed. And what my feed feeds me is *lack*. It doesn't show me more. It spotlights what I'm missing in my life, like an algorithm tailored to my ache.

Being super-connected somehow makes me feel disconnected.

The very simple truth that we don't want to admit to ourselves is that we feel truly lonely at times. Throughout the day. In the night. It makes us feel guilty. Because why should we feel lonely when we aren't really alone? Kids hanging on our legs and husbands at home at night. And, above all, an ever-present Friend living within.

The fact is you can feel alone together.

I often feel lonely. And I always feel guilty about it.

I buy the lie over and again that perhaps a scroll, a retweet, or a "like" might lessen the ache. It doesn't. It won't. It's merely a cheap purchase from a store that doesn't accept returns. It's the fast food of connection, and I keep returning to the drive-through where they say, "Welcome back."

Maybe I am not alone in this?

After many moments of aching loneliness, I can tell you that scrolling makes the loneliness larger than life. Studying Facebook statuses puts you in a numb-like state. And lingering online makes you face the chasm of comparing.

For a long time, I guarded myself from the comparing that

comes from the social media stare. I kept gratefulness at the forefront of my mind, careful to give thanks for what was good in my life. I'd never been the jealous type. More the "I'm so happy for you" and "let's be friends" girl.

But algorithms get smarter. The enemy of our soul knows how to market to our ache. God gives us eyes to see what is good, the gifts we've been given; the enemy's agenda is to get us to look through the lens of lack. To have us focus and fixate on what we do not have and to envy what others do.

Over time I began looking through the lens of:

How does she keep her house so clean? OK, I'm no stranger to how this works. The mess is cropped out. The filter is HB1 with the brightness and contrast bumped up. But she always shares about how she lives so minimally. Her life is so ordered. Mine is out of control.

They are in Europe now? Everyone is going to Europe these days. I bet they got their airline tickets sponsored on Icelandair. I wish I were back in England. No, Scotland. Maybe Holland...I wish I was anywhere but here.

Do they dote like this IRL? If he says how amazing and hot his wife is one more time, I'm gonna throw up in my mouth a little. Get a room. Like gag me with a spoon....I wonder if I would feel nauseated if my husband said that about me publicly.

Could it have been? Her dad is teaching her son how to sail on the family vacation they take every year, in the spot they've been going to since she was a kid. He comes by for dinner. He pours out his wisdom like wine at a wedding. I never thought the thing I'd be most Instagram jealous of would be undivided attention and memory making. You know, how it is "supposed" to be, *Growing Pains* style—everyone playing the roles they were supposed to play.

My ache only got achier.

———— ....

We met by the snowbank to exchange English tea and Buzz Lightyear toys, Jen and I.

It felt like minus-20 degrees that morning. Not an exaggeration—it was actually what my iPhone app read, along with "Fair." It is anything but. Life is not fair, and neither is the weather, I've learned.

HEAVY HEARTS ARE NOT SO HEAVY WHEN WE SHARE THEM WITH A FRIEND.

Our two bus-long cars convened side by side, facing a small mountain of dirty snow, and Jen jumped into my car. It was too cold to stand outside and pass bags through the car windows.

We've been friends for a very long time. I've known Jen since I was in the fourth grade. This past year we have been passing things back and forth. Family to family.

"These don't fit Connor any longer. Would Luke like these ATV-riding pants?"

"Yes, thank you!"

"This Buzz Lightyear costume has just been hanging in Rocco's closet. Do you want it for Pax?"

"He would love it!" We both hope it fits.

She handed me the tea, and I gave her more Buzz Lightyear gear. "How are you?" Jen asks, smiling her happy smile.

"Good. Good." But I didn't mean it. It's just that I didn't mean to unload anything but the toys from my basement. I tried to fake it because I've fed on the food for thought that says, "Keep it together"—that I shouldn't be a bother. For a lifetime, I've filled my plate from someone else's "should and shouldn't" buffet. But, lately, it's beginning to taste bitter—off. I'm really not one for keeping up appearances, yet instinctively I don't want to appear like I'm falling apart. But the truth is I *do* feel like I'm falling apart a lot of the time.

I fake it. I feel like a knockoff Louis Vuitton—an imitation of myself—and I cringe. "Good. Good." I flounder..."Not good. Life has been overwhelming lately." I let Jen see past the exterior. Slowly, I'm learning that there are times when it is best to not "keep it all together." And also that there are friends who will not love you any less because of it.

There were tears. There was truth telling. And then there was prayer.

As I opened myself up to true connection and friendship, I allowed myself to become the friend I want to be for others. To allow others to greet me with the same kind of empathy and understanding I am learning to give. I don't ever want a friend to hide their hurting heart from me by putting on a fake face.

I drove home and made a cup of the tea, with one sugar and coconut milk creamer. I nursed my Harrods' brew and thought, *Maybe I said too much. Maybe I am too much.* I told my thoughts to be quiet, and with each sip I more fully filled my spirit with this truth: Heavy hearts are not so heavy when we share them with a friend. When we keep everything to ourselves, even if our intentions are good—not to burden or weigh down others—then we are choosing to weigh ourselves down with a weight that will eventually crush us.

Logging on to look for *something* disconnects us from what we have. From *whom* we have. Connecting IRL disconnects us from the chat rooms, the trolling, the world wide web of our minds.

Sometimes friendship looks more like carrying tea in your suitcase over an ocean and exchanging Buzz Lightyear toys in the parking lot for prayer than a styled selfie at brunch published on social media.

I think about the times I've felt alone in my life. My journals confirm tales of it as a teenager and into my twenties. I wasn't alone, truly. I had parents who loved me. I had friends to hang out with. I had youth leaders who mentored me. I sometimes had a boyfriend. Yet there were times I sat out and stayed at home. Hiccups in teenage friendships. Breakups that left me wounded. I'd hibernate on my island waterbed, listening to the *Edward Scissorhands* soundtrack, melancholic music for the mood. Eventually someone would call—an invitation out of the basement, out of myself. Sometimes I would emerge. And sometimes I'd decline, make up an excuse, say, "Maybe tomorrow." I couldn't even fake it back then.

These days, I take into account my personality type, the wiring of my very own world wide web. Strangely, the results of a multiple-choice introspective personality test, such as the Myers–Briggs Type Indicator, know me better than I know myself. The questions I answered labeled me as an INFJ. The results state that INFJs are rare. It attests they tend to *feel* very lonely, but not from lack of human presence or relationships; rather, they *feel* alone in their minds and often *feel* out of place. My type longs to be understood (don't we all?). Knowing this helps me to accept that while my personality may be rare, I am not alone. And maybe more importantly, it helps me to see one word consistently repeated. A word I've worn, like spots on a leopard:

feel
/fēl/
verb
1. to make itself perceived or apparent; seem[2]

I have a strong propensity to perceive (my husband concurs) the good and the bad. Phaedrus said, "Things aren't always what they seem."[3] I'm learning this also pertains to my own thinking and perceptions.

My youth pastor, Jeanne Mayo, used to say, "Loneliness is God's cry for intimacy," and then always followed up with, "Turn loneliness into alone time with God." I followed those words. I followed them at fifteen and all the way to thirty-nine, where I've found it to be, "Loneliness is an *opportunity* for intimacy with God." And this has always been the balm to the ache. The only square in the feed that feeds. The truth to the lie. I am not alone. I may *feel* lonely, but I am not alone.

You may *feel* lonely, but you are not alone.

Jesus felt loneliness. But He was not alone.

We are not alone in this.

"We don't have a priest who is out of touch with our reality. He's been through weakness and testing, experienced it all—all but the sin. So let's walk right up to him and get what he is so ready to give. Take the mercy, accept the help" (Heb. 4:15–16 MSG).

Knowing that the Savior of all mankind experienced what you are going through—what you feel—is a beautiful offering. Yet He offers even more. He offers to *never* leave you or forsake you. His very presence says, "Come to me and receive what I am so ready to give. What has already been given. Myself" (1 Tim. 2:6 NLT).

He is "A father of the fatherless and a judge *and* protector to the widows, *I make a home for the lonely*" (Ps. 68:5–6 AMP, emphasis added).

Kids hanging on our legs and husbands home at night. And, above all, *an ever-present Friend living within.* We have a Father, a Protector, and a Home.

These days I trade: Guilt for grace. Loneliness for alone time with God. A lie for the truth. Online for IRL. I feast on grace, and it nourishes me. I hear the heart of the Father, and it isn't saying, "Welcome back." It says, "I've never left, and I never will."

———— ....

Wouldn't it be the most obvious plot of the enemy to make us *feel* alone when the truth is we are *never* alone? There is no separation. Nothing can separate us from Christ (Rom. 8:35–38 NLT). How can we be separated when we are in Him and He is in us? But how the enemy wants us to *feel* alone. To let our emotions speak louder than the truth of our hearts, where Christ is at home.

Loneliness is a separation problem. It is not about being alone. It is about *feeling* separated. Freedom comes by love—as it always does. NO-THING can separate us from the love of Christ.

What if we stare it down for what it is and skip the screen? Write it out. Work it out. Pray. Believe the truth. Deny the lie. Call a friend. Be a friend. Even if it feels forced. And that connection? It will turn into communion.

the col
of soul
stretch

CHAPTER ELEVEN | THE COLOR OF SOUL STRETCHING

ELEVEN

"We throw open our doors to God and discover at the same moment that he has already thrown open his door to us. We find ourselves standing where we always hoped we might stand—out in the wide open spaces of God's grace and glory, standing tall and shouting praise."

—ROMANS 5:2 (MSG)

Life can often feel boxed in. Tight. Even smothering. Caged and controlled. It sounds startling, but I bet you've felt it. Like your soul is cramped and all you want is to stretch—stretch your limbs and stretch your soul.

I found a little extra space for my soul in color.

It's common for my kids to ask, "Mom, what's your favorite color?" And before I can answer, they usually do for me: "I know, I know! Your favorite color is white." I suppose if you visited my blog, you might come to that conclusion too.

I don't know how white became such a favorite of mine. But at some point I was drawn to it. The crisp cleanness of it. The blank canvas feel of it. Perhaps it started when I first happened upon *Shabby Chic*, wandering around Barnes & Noble on a Saturday afternoon. It was the first interior design book that had ever caught my eye. I'd always loved old things and favored pastels, and it was as if I had discovered their mate—white. White paint. White textiles. White furniture. I think what I loved most was that white meant possibility and that when I looked at it and when I lived within it, I felt its spaciousness. I felt its light.

——— ....

This discovery came during a time when my husband, Stephen, and I were purchasing our first home in Atlanta, land of the big, beautiful homes. I pictured us in a cute, cottage-like first home. What we ended up with was an oversized cookie-cutter house with a two-story great room and more rooms than we needed for just the two of us. I remember feeling physical pressure to get the home decorated—like a weight on my chest, a breathlessness. Every room needed to be completed and every corner embellished, as if it were the model home for showing. That's how it was done in the South, or at least that was this out-of-place Midwesterner's impression. Every home picture-perfect.

At the time, I didn't know what I was doing when it came to decorating. I didn't have the energy, drive, or even desire to do it all at once. And I certainly didn't have the money. At twenty-two, I wasn't sure of myself, let alone my style.

I incorporated toile because everyone else did. I didn't even know what toile was until I saw it in my friend Robin's home. Stephen and I painted the dining room a deep maroon not because I liked it but because that was the trend. I assumed my windows shouldn't be bare because my friend Rebekah had all of her windows adorned with window treatments she had sewn herself. My mother-in-law confirmed that my windows were in need of covering, and she kindly made me fancy floral window treatments, asking me if I wanted swags or scallops or pinch pleats or pockets. I had no idea what any of that meant.

"I THINK IT IS IMPORTANT TO *REMOVE* ANYTHING YOU DON'T LIKE FROM A HOME AND START WITH A CLEAN SLATE."

In all of this confusion, however, I did choose to go with white kitchen cabinets. Everyone tried to talk me out of them, saying, "White cabinets are so five years ago." At the time, everyone was opting for richer, darker cabinetry. But for once in my life, I didn't budge. Somewhere deep down, I knew what I really liked. And so, our kitchen was very white and very bright, and I was happy with it. The only other room in that house that felt like me was a little office with French doors that I turned into a makeshift sunroom. With birthday money, I bought a beat-up potting table made of rusty metal and a section of an old picket fence. I purchased a wicker chair from Pier 1 and put a jute geometric rug underneath it all. I loved that odd, out-of-place room. It felt like an expression of myself. I felt the most at home in it.

I learned *that* is what a home *should* look like: an expression of those who live within. Your home should be a livable reflection of you. When someone walks into your home, they should find that it complements you. That it is an extension of your personality. Your home doesn't just house you; it houses your story.

———— ....

Eventually, life led us back to the Midwest. After another cookie-cutter home, this time in Chicago, we ended up in my childhood home. For a good year or two, I felt the need to decorate around the style of the home. The way that it was and how it had always been gave me the itch: dark colors, old furniture my parents left behind, and anything Pottery Barn that I had impulsively purchased to perk up the place. After painting a pumpkin-orange accent wall in our family room, which turned out to be more basketball-orange, I knew something had to change, starting with the paint that hadn't yet dried on the wall.

Around the same time, I toured the magical home of Annie Smith, who owns Euro Trash, a design firm that imports unique décor finds from Europe. After meeting Annie, visiting her home, and learning about her business, I asked if I could interview her for my blog. She kindly agreed. "What is the best room to start decorating in a home?" I asked her.

While I had never adhered to decorating one room at a time, I thought surely I was doing something wrong by purchasing random things that caught my eye instead of focusing on one space at a time and completing it. I assumed Annie's golden answer would both correct and advise me.

Instead, she surprised me and said: "I would like to answer this question in a different way. I think it is important to *remove* anything you don't like from a home and start with a clean slate. Don't 'do one room' then move to the next. I would rather live sparsely in a home and have the whole thing come together slowly than have the jarring feeling of a new style against the old. In my own home, I spent about a year 'undecorating.' I don't concentrate on one room at a time. Opportunity also plays a big role. If I find a drop-dead gorgeous piece for the living room for a good price, I will buy it. I wouldn't look at it and think, 'Well, I am looking for a dining table right now.' The dining table could be plywood covered in fabric until the right one came along. If the opportunity is there, grab it!"

Her answer encouraged me. Instead of being corrected, I was cut loose. After our chat, I went on a self-appointed mission to de-brownify my home. Everything in our new home felt dark and drab, and it was suffocating me.

Undecorate.

Start with a clean slate. Give yourself room to stretch.

It's OK to focus on more than one room.

Instead of adding, I needed to empty. Instead of color, I needed a whitewash.

Any person looking in would think the opposite. "Take it one room at a time. What a great start. This style suits your home nicely. Keep going. Add. Decorate. Adorn."

Isn't it this way in our lives, too?

I think the Lord provides us opportunities to look at our lives, to peer into the windows of the home of our hearts, as He asks, "Is this what you really want? Is this you? Why have you filled your home with this? Would you like more space? More light?"

YOU MIGHT BE REALLY ATTACHED TO THE 1980S WALLPAPER THAT HAS COVERED THE HURT IN YOUR HEART SINCE YOU WERE EIGHT.

Many times the life we find ourselves in reflects someone else's design. Someone else's dreams for us. Someone else's choices that affected us. Or perhaps it is just a picture of what we settle for—a home full of hand-me-downs.

And the funny thing is, we can be so protective and possessive about things that don't suit us and are ill-fitting just because we think they are ours. Just because they are something to hold. Something to have.

Are there things in your life that are suffocating you? Things that take up space and don't allow room for what you really want or what God would like to add to it?

I'm sure there are times you honestly do not know what you want and so it's easier to keep things the same. Feeling boxed in, cramped, and even caged becomes familiar and normal. Although you've grown accustomed to your tight space, maybe even convinced yourself that it's cozy, I bet your soul is ready for a good stretch. Sometimes you need a glimpse of spaciousness—to take it in with your own eyes—before you make a choice to live it out in your own life.

I've found that when I make space, when I empty out what needs to go, I feel more alive, open to possibility, free to be creative, ready to begin anew.

So, get rid of what is ill-fitting, what you don't like. Then stand back. You'll realize there is still so much that needs to change, even if you can't put your finger on it yet. You'll start to give thought to what you want to replace or consider bringing back what you removed. There are many sparse spots. So, sit with them. Live with them. And most importantly, ask the Designer of your life, "What needs to go next?" He knows. You might not like His response. You might be really attached to the 1980s wallpaper that has covered the hurt in your heart since you were eight. You know the pattern, the feel, the faded colors so well. You can't bear to remove the outdated wallpaper because as tired of it as you are, you can't imagine not seeing it anymore. It's ugly but so familiar. You can't even remember what your heart looked liked before it was covered. Is it difficult to picture something new in its place? The thought of removing it sounds arduous at best. The peeling away is painful. Stripping, peeling, pulling, tugging at a thirty-year-old patch job.

I'm peeling away the paper in my life, even today. The pattern is colored in security, safety, and familiarity. And it's not coming off easily. The adhesive is so strong. The tearing agonizing. But the Designer is patient as I take the time to look behind each layer and to let go. He is working alongside me. He hasn't left me to the task alone. I have no idea what the new pattern will be. I'm not at that stage. But I know I don't want to stay in the tight places. My soul knows what it feels like to stretch. "This spacious, free life is from God, it's also protected, safe, and God-strengthened (Ps. 37:39–40 MSG)." I no longer fear wide-open spaces. I long for them. It's where I stride freely as I look for God's truth and wisdom (Ps. 119 MSG).

Sometimes we must sit bare for a season.

Sometimes we must sit empty for a time.

But the truth is…

What is bare will be covered.

What is empty will be filled.

The Designer of your life knows exactly what suits you. He knows the colors of your life, what will give you comfort, what will inspire you, what will move you, what will cover and fill you.

White is not a color, they tell me. "Pick another favorite, Mom."

I disagree. And being the Internet girl I am, I had to ask Google, "Is white a color?" I typed fast and furiously for my answer.

And this was what I found: *In physics, color is defined as visible light with a wavelength. White doesn't have a specific wavelength. White contains all visible wavelengths of light. White is the blending of all colors. There is a theory called the additive color theory that states that the sum of all colors of light add up to white.*[1]

White is all colors. White is light.

This is why I love it so, why I am drawn to it. I love white because I love light. And in my life I want to let in as much light as possible. I want to let its glowing rays peer into every dark corner and color my whole life.

———— ....

In your life, home may need more work than your heart. Or maybe it's the other way around. Sometimes it's both. But as you work with your hands to make physical space, the Spirit will speak to you about the space He'd like to make in the home of your heart.

If you're ready to freshen your home, you don't have to empty out your entire house and paint all the walls white. Unless, of course, you want to. I wasn't able to empty everything out. I still had to live with some hand-me-downs, but only the ones I liked or that had meaning. I wasn't able to overhaul the busy, brown, newly remodeled kitchen. But I changed what I could, painted when I could. We sold our two-year-old brown couch on Craigslist and replaced it with a white hand-me-down sofa that reminds me of my mom falling asleep to *Frasier* every night (I still haven't found my dream sofa). Eleven years later, the kitchen still feels out of place in my house. But I decided it was better that the kitchen feel out of place than me.

If it is your heart home that needs refreshing, let me offer you a few ways to stretch your soul.

01 /   Empty your heart out before God, the Designer of your life. For some, that takes the form of prayer. Many times, for me, it begins with a pen and my journal. Simply share with Him what is taking up space and making you feel suffocated in life. Tell Him of your desire to live a spacious, God-protected life, striding freely with Him in wide-open spaces.

02 /   Ask the Spirit to reveal what is taking up space that you might not even be aware of.

03 /   Ask God to show you or remind you of His design for your life.

04 /   Allow Him to cover what is bare and to fill what is empty. Give Him permission to add to and adorn your heart home.

If it is your physical home, here are some ways to make space and undecorate your house.

01 / Get rid of anything that you don't find beautiful.

02 / Get rid of anything that doesn't make you happy.

03 / Get rid of anything that you don't find useful.

04 / Get rid of anything that makes you feel stressed.

05 / If something doesn't have a place, maybe it doesn't have a place.

06 / Ask yourself, "Do I need two of that?"

07 / Pick a base color for your house and create consistency throughout your hallways and main living areas (whether it be white, gray, or any neutral that suits you).

If you would like to paint a space and are drawn to white, like me, here are a few of my favorite shades:

+ Ultra White / Dutch Boy

+ Pure White / Sherwin Williams

+ Eider White / Sherwin Williams

+ Cotton Balls / Benjamin Moore OC-122 (great for ceilings if you aren't using bright white)

+ Winter Wheat / Benjamin Moore 232 (a soft off-white that I use throughout my home as bright white doesn't work)

CHAPTER TWELVE | WHAT THE TREES TELL ME

TWELVE

When I am among the trees,
I would almost say that they save me, and daily.
—MARY OLIVER, "WHEN I AM AMONG THE TREES"[1]

In summertime, my backyard is lush and green. The edges and borders dance with flowers: purple coneflowers, black-eyed Susans, hostas, and daylilies, to name a few. I see it as a secret garden of sorts, a fortress that holds the fun of twenty-five summers. The tall evergreens and ash trees with their diamond-patterned bark have always seemed to wave and bend and nod and whisper to me. And, if I'm lucky, sometimes I catch the conversation.

Psithurism,[2] I read, is the sound of the wind in the trees.

They seem like people to me, the trees in my backyard.

There is a black walnut tree by the office door and, adjacent to it, a hawthorn, to which our hammock is coupled. They almost meet in the middle, branches reaching out toward each other, but there is space between them. A tall Norway spruce with long bending arms stands behind them both. Its elderly limbs point to true north; when the wind rushes through, it takes a humble bow. And on a warm summer day, I've seen it waving and gesturing, "Come, come," as we do with a fold of the hand. I'm not sure what the breeze is carrying, but those trees—they are trying to tell me something.

———— ....

The other week I was walking through my wooded neighborhood for exercise, for stress relief, for quiet, for creativity. I began a familiar daydream that goes like this... *How nice it would be to live near mountains or the ocean or some overwhelming form of nature.* I think of all of the time I've spent in Colorado, Arizona, and California and how every time I visit I ask myself the same questions: "Do people who live here take this view, this beauty, for granted? Do they even notice the mountains out their windows anymore? Are they as accustomed to the ocean as I am to cornfields?" And just before I get carried away in conversation with myself, I round the corner and find myself nestled under a canopy of trees. In that instant, I realized what I had not been seeing out my own window: the woods are my overwhelming form of nature, my Midwestern wonder—God's offering of nature to me.

Trees, I once heard, represent rest. And here, without realizing it, I've been neighboring with respite.

I can never decide when I like them best. Every year, each season, I try to decide again and again. I judge what the woods wear, as if I'm a regular on *Project Runway*. Autumn is pushing for first place with all of its colors and crunch. Summer is a shoo-in for second with its wealth of green, stately and regal, emanating a fairy-tale feel. Spring is a serious competitor with its miniature buds because when they bloom, pinks and yellows burst forth and fragrances float through the back door, so that I only faintly remember fall's luster, like last night's dream. And winter. Can it even compete? The trees are bare and dead. Yet every year I declare winter the winner and give those trees the reigning title: "Most beautiful."

BEAUTY IS NOT ABOUT STAYING THE SAME; OFTEN BEAUTY IS BEST DISPLAYED IN CHANGE.

They aren't crowned with their own clothing during the cold months. Most days they stand bare and brown and lifeless, even sad. But on very special days when the air is just right, heaven's hush falls from the sky and dresses each tree in a custom white gown. Within hours, my small, simple town is transformed into Narnia.

I read once that trees do not have to keep all of their cells from freezing in the winter, only the living ones. The trees begin their work in the fall by sweetening fluids within the living cells, acting as an antifreeze and making the cells more pliable. They are squeezed but said not to puncture among the expanding ice, among the pressure. The tree's main focus for subzero survival is to not allow the living cells to freeze.[3]

As I write this, it is now winter, and there is a barren white ash tree and two Norway spruce trees in view. They are thriving, and I think about how they have not allowed their living cells to freeze, a life-giving work happening within that can't be seen with the naked eye. We must do the same. In my very long winter, I have felt the biting cold, so frigid it burns like the January air in Chicago. I've felt the choke of grief and the physical pressure of anxiety that left me feeling like the walking dead but for the living cells—but for Jesus.

THIS WORK TAKING PLACE *IN* US IS OF FAR GREATER IMPORTANCE AND WORTH TO GOD THAN THE WORK WE PRODUCE.

The living Jesus in me made me pliable even when it appeared that I was brittle, ready to snap like a branch. Like within the trees, there is a deep work that happens within, when we allow it. It's a quiet work that consists of the living cells, Jesus, moving in and out of the dead places, sending the sweet fluids—the refreshment—to the most parched places of your heart. For me, this work has produced a change that has gone as deep as my roots.

This work taking place *in* us is of far greater importance and worth to God than the work we produce. Yet the work within always coincides with the work that comes out of us. And the God of peace equips us with everything good that we may do His will (Heb. 13:20–21, paraphrase).

In this season, I'm learning to welcome the covering of another. I accept heaven's clothing as the holy gift that it is. I wear the adoration of the heavens and in dormancy allow Jesus to protect my living cells. In receiving this gift, I warm to the truth of the coming spring, in the promise of bearing fruit, in the fragrance of new life. And I remember how in the season of fully flourishing, I didn't wear the covering of another; I provided it. I offered shade and a place for others to rest and find refreshment. And I will again.

———— ....

"Come, come," I hear the trees whisper, waving in distant warmth.

I read over and again: "My beloved is to me the most fragrant apple tree—he stands above the sons of men. Sitting under his grace-shadow, I blossom in his shade" (Song of Songs 2:3 TPT). I'm certain the "something" the trees have been saying to me is that is no matter the season, God's grace-shadow is available, always, to cover me.

Today, in the stillness of a January fog, I hear the trees whisper, "Beauty is not about staying the same; often beauty is best displayed in change."

Things the trees have whispered to me

01 /   Accept the offering of beauty where you are, as you are.

02 /   Wave in the wind, but remain unwavering.

03 /   Embrace change in each season and its purpose.

04 /   Rest is to be received and reciprocated to those in need.

05 /   God's presence and influence upon your inner life are what give way to flourishing.

06 /   Notice beauty in its abundance, and look for it in the barrenness.

PART TWO

CHAPTER THIRTEEN | THE COTTAGE BY THE SEA

THIRTEEN

He is wooing you from the jaws of distress to
a spacious place free from restriction, to the comfort
of your table laden with choice food.

—JOB 36:13 (NIV)

---

ately I have this recurring daydream. It varies, and
with each reverie the details become more full.
It starts with a cottage, tucked in a wild but managed English flowering garden. Roses. Foxgloves. Lilies of
the valley. Daisies. Hollyhocks. Wisterias, everywhere. Just
beyond the garden, on the other side of the picket fence,
are rolling hills that surround the house. And, beyond the
hills, within walking distance are stunning cliffs with the sea
bellowing below. You can hear the sea from the cottage,
ever so slightly like a lullaby. I haven't worked out the inside
of the cottage yet. But I know that it is painted white and
there is an old stone fireplace with a writing desk nearby,

complete with an old clickety-clackety typewriter atop. It feels both cozy and spacious. And if I open a window, I can smell the sea.

I'd been dreaming of a writing refuge long before the cottage by the sea. A place of my own, in my backyard. A shed, a shack, anything with four walls and a roof would do. I'm certain that with a can of paint, a desk, and the whisper of trees I can find and create beauty. I'm convinced that this will help in the healing of my heart and the quieting of my mind. This place will be a suture for my soul. A sure place of repair and reprieve.

I returned to counseling not too long ago, really ready this time to do the hard work of healing, which I've come to believe involves inviting the Father, myself, and others into my wounds, over and over again, until the wounds can be defined. Then I can at last receive the healing and freedom that Christ already purchased.

Instead of focusing on my situation at hand, my counselor wanted to look further back, to look for underlying pain, to see what I had been carrying not just for the past six years but since I was a little six-year-old girl. If I'm honest, this is why I didn't want to go to counseling. I wasn't interested in digging into memories or parts of my heart that I'd kept at bay for all my life. But she said we needed to start at the beginning, to dislodge what has been woven into the fabric of my being—things that I don't even realize are there until something disrupts the peace and triggers those tiny hairline fractures to feel great twinges of pain.

So, together, we traveled from 1977 to 2016 and sometimes

stopped in 1983. Always, we ended up in today. At the end of one visit, she asked me to picture a place where I felt most safe. I said I didn't have a place other than my house. She said, "It has to be anywhere but your house." It was there on the counselor's couch that I first envisioned the cottage by the sea.

I'm convinced that we all must have a place where we can be quiet and contemplate beauty, even in—especially in— our brokenness. A place where all the noise goes quiet, our senses sit still, and we can take in and express beauty however we do that best.

Over time, my bedroom became that place for me. It's not the writing cottage by the sea, painted white on the inside, with ivy crawling up the outside. Rather, it's a room between two rooms, a rectangular hallway, a walkway to my husband's office. But it's the closest thing I have to my own sacred space.

I spend a significant amount of time in my room. It's where I read, sitting in my husband's grandma's blue velvet chair tucked in the corner, with a bookshelf behind me and books piling up on the floor beside me. It's where I roll out my yoga mat and stretch or do Pilates. It's where I write at my Parsons desk in front of a recently half-painted pink wall that I thought would inspire me (it does). It's where I shut the door, after telling everyone to stay out. It's wear I cuddle and watch TV, after inviting everyone in.

It's not a perfect place, not even ideal, but it does the job. And on the days when it doesn't, I drive to Starbucks to write or I go into my closet and curl up on the floor to pray and pour out my heart—just me, Jesus, and all my clothes. I go in there to hide away.

I don't think it's any coincidence that we all long for a safe place. A hiding place. A quiet place. A secret place. An inspiring place. A place of our own. I believe it's an innate longing. I read over and over in the Psalms how David was looking for, asking for, the same. A king who had a palace was still in search of a place. "I run for dear life to you, my safe place," David sang (Ps. 16:1 TPT). "I trust you, Lord, to be my hiding place" he said (Ps. 31:1 TPT).

And the beauty is that he found this place, before a crown and a kingdom offered him everything. He found this place outside decorated walls, while in the fields tending sheep, while in a cave, scared for his life, hiding from his enemies.

The Lord gave him peace in the field and in the cave, among his troubles and his enemies, long before He gave him peace in the palace. Later in his life, David looks around at his palace and is troubled that the Lord's place is a tent (where the Ark of the Covenant resided). The Lord asks him, "Will you build Me a house to live in?" It becomes David's dream to give the Lord a place. God then goes on to tell David that He will choose a place for his people (Israel) and plant them so they can live in their own homes (2 Sam. 7:5, 10 NCV). David doesn't see the completion of the temple—of

the home—but his son Solomon fulfills the dream, the promise of a place.

God had been David's place. What an honor for him to then give God a place. I think our story is the same. Same weary souls looking for a safe place and the same God looking for a place to dwell. It's an offering going both ways.

God offers us a place; He has "always been our eternal home, our hiding place from generation to generation" (Ps. 90:1 TPT). In return we can offer ourselves as a living home.

There was one more thing I envisioned in the cottage by the sea. Jesus. He was trying to embrace me, but I was fighting His love, wanting to cover my wounds instead of embracing His healing. Kicking and hitting and pushing Him away like a toddler having a tantrum over a parent offering ice cream. Finally exhausted, I rested in His strong arms and received. We both sat down: me at the desk and Him in a comfortable leather chair across from me. He sat watching with kind eyes while I typed, as if He had all the time in the world.

Click-ca-Click-ca-Click-ca-Click. Click. Click. Ding.

Return.

I pulled the paper, which read like a journal entry, from the typewriter and handed it over. He read it as if it was the most interesting thing in the world. And then He just sat with me.

It would be wonderful to have a little cottage with an

English garden by the sea. But the place I dream of now is a person. Jesus is my place. He is my home.

Finding a place of your own

01 / Select a space; even the corner of a room will do.

02 / Decorate said space as little or as much as you like. Add what inspires you: books, art, photos, paint, a cozy chair, a table or desk.

03 / If you can't find a space or if what you've found is less than ideal at times, retreat to a closet.

04 / Ask God to be your home. Find in Him a hiding place. Trust Him to be your safe place.

05 / Be prepared for ideas, dreams, creativity, and beauty to originate in this place.

06 / Visit this place of your own as often as you like.

07 / You may go to get lost. You will always be found.

a messy
& life

CHAPTER FOURTEEN | A MESSY HOUSE AND LIFE

house

FOURTEEN

"A perfectly kept house is the sign of a misspent life."

—MARY RANDOLPH CARTER, *A PERFECTLY KEPT HOUSE IS THE SIGN OF A MISSPENT LIFE*[1]

My floors are covered in crumbs most of the time. I'm not extremely vigilant about this except for in the summer when I find myself battling armies of ants. It's war with the ants or wield the broom, and I prefer the latter of the two. I'm also attentive to the floor when company comes over. Because if I can't keep the crumbs off the floor, then could it be a sign that I can't keep my life together? Sometimes I believe ridiculous things.

Anyways, if it's not crumbs, it's toys.

You too?

Thanks to my years as an administrative assistant color-coding files, I've always been an organized person. But with the birth of each child, I've lost a little part of that self. I've had to let a portion of her go. Well, let me be honest, it wasn't really a letting go. It was a struggle, a kung fu fight with myself, a game of tug-of-war to hold on to the me I thought I've always been—the me I want to be.

I just want a little order. Is there anything wrong with that?

I try to be realistic. I understand that with six people in a house, the work is never going to be done. If the house is clean, then I can assure you closets are not. If the laundry is washed and folded, then I can promise there is a dirty pair of Captain America underwear wadded up behind the garbage can in the bathroom. (I've discovered them there more times than I care to admit.) The minute the toys are put away, someone dumps a box of Legos onto our living room floor. When we finish cleaning up one meal, it feels like only minutes until we are preparing the next. And almost always, when the sheets have been changed, someone has a wet accident that night.

My wise mom has been saying the same thing to me day after day, year after year, baby after baby: "Trina, you are wasting precious time. Your children aren't going to remember a perfectly clean house; they are going to remember a present mother. You are going to miss all of this."

Her words are my inner voice, only I can't seem to heed them. I still struggle and fight myself. I listen to wisdom, but then I look at Pinterest, blogs, and glossy magazines. I let the styled images speak to me as if they are real life, even though I know they are not. I know firsthand what goes into the perfection of that 600x400-pixel Photoshopped photo: a brand's beautiful product, props, a professional stylist, a photographer, lighting, and editing. I remind myself that on the other side of the lens, in the adjoining room, there are piles and baskets and remnants of real life that aren't pretty enough to make the cut—just like at my house.

WHEN WE LOOK TO IMAGES FOR ANYTHING MORE THAN INSPIRATION AND IDEAS, WE RISK DAMAGING OUR REAL LIFE FOR SOMETHING THAT IS NOT REAL.

Pinterest, blogs, magazines, and Instagram squares, which I very much enjoy finding and sharing, are not bad in and of themselves, but they cannot be the standard to which we compare ourselves. When we look to images for anything more than inspiration and ideas, we risk damaging our real life for something that is not real. When our gaze shifts from information and inspiration to discontentment and dissat- isfaction, the glow of the screen has not enlightened us. Rather, it has darkened our view, dulled our ability to see beauty, and hindered our chance to experience it tangibly. So easy to agree with yet hard to live by.

On my worst days (say, when I'm already anxious about keeping up with the everyday schedule of six people and then receive a stressful phone call), I have an insatiable desire to keep my house clean. I take on this clean-freak persona that takes no prisoners if you're in my line of sight. Those around me get the look of a deer in headlights. I am the truck coming full speed ahead to tuck the deer—I mean kids—in bed. And the only thing I can focus on is the globs of toothpaste all over the bathroom counter; the drawers we organized the day before, now bursting with clothes; an overflowing hamper that was empty only hours earlier; and enough half-consumed water bottles to build a fortress for our entire stuffed animal collection. I don't just focus on it; I nag about it. I rush through bedtime prayers and wonder what I'm doing wrong that my kids cannot keep their rooms clean. *Am I not training them right? Do we need to get rid of more things? Why can't I fully embrace this minimalistic lifestyle?* My mind runs wild.

I'm fighting to not lose another fraction of myself, and I justify it with *I'm just trying to keep my home running. If I don't keep things moving, who will?*

I just want a little control. Is there anything so wrong with that?

Cue kung fu kick.

When things around me become more and more out of control, I *crave* order like a pregnant lady craves mint chocolate chip ice cream. I want things under control, preferably my way. I want some order back, and I'll take it however I can get it. Even if it comes by way of clean floors and shining countertops. Even if it comes by ordering around my little ones to clean out the clutter under their beds and to scrub the scum in the bathroom.

It is only after fourteen years as a parent, and six years into my life feeling totally out of control, that I finally see what is wrong with my response. For one, the cycle is exhausting. And trying to stay in complete control, even of one's own home, is arduous.

In trying to force order (i.e., cleaning any kind of mess and fixing anything that is broken), I'm fixing my gaze on all that is wrong. I'm looking through the filter of all that needs fixing. And then I miss the beauty that is right in front of me. I miss out on hearing the beauty in the munchkin voice saying prayers at bedtime and asking for one more back scratch and song. I miss seeing fully the first-grade toothless grin and the sparkle of innocence in the big blue eyes. I fail to notice the invitation to listen when my fourteen-year-old wants to gab. I'm blinded by the clothes on the floor and the laundry I still need to fold. I fail to see what is right and what is good.

There is nothing wrong with cleaning to relieve stress (I know many women who do this) or organizing to relieve mental clutter. But when we employ these activities to achieve control, we are only setting ourselves up to lose more of it. The truth is I can't control anything. And neither can you. Accepting this truth is equivalent to a deep clean. So give it over to God. Find freedom in letting go.

Every year, when we take a trip with our friends, we stay in a house together. It always starts out clean, and then within a day weird things begin to happen, like shoes on the counter, Walmart bags filled with sea shells at the front door, or cactus clippings crumpled up beside the sea-salt-and-cracked-pepper-chip bag. And mixed-up piles of twelve people's things everywhere. We do the dishes and we wash clothes, but we let the rest go until the end of the week when we all work together to clean the place up. I don't know if it's because I'm in vacation mode or because it's not my house or because I truly have no control. But whatever it is, I *love* it. I love leaving Rocco's shoes on the counter while we watch TV or heading out the door for an impromptu Starbucks run with breakfast dishes in the sink.

Why can't I be vacation-Trina at home? I wouldn't go for shoes on the counter, but I think I could learn to let the dishes soak.

If I go to a girlfriend's house and see a mess, I let out a sigh of relief. I don't judge the junk mail piled on the counter, the coats and the book bags scattered on the floor, or the groceries yet to be put away. I see her house as lived-in and the hub of five lives. I feel at home.

I visit another girlfriend whose house is immaculate and wonder what she thinks when she comes to my house. How does she keep it all so clean? Does she really keep it that clean all the time? Maybe she just runs around like a madwoman before guests arrive, like I do.

I want to run around less like a madwoman. I want to remind myself that my piles make others feel at home.

Last night there were two globby Star Wars toothpaste tubes on the counter. I chucked one in the can (I can't be sure if any Captain America underwear were behind it because I didn't look) and stepped over the clothes on the floor (clean or dirty is anyone's guess). Then I nestled on the bottom bunk with Liam. I told him we had to tidy up tomorrow because we should. I listened to facts about Steph Curry. (His real name is Wardell, FYI.) And I relaxed because those dirty clothes in the bathroom had nothing on his Chiclet-tooth grin.

Slowly I'm learning to live life among the mess and the magic, and it almost looks like vacation.

CHAPTER FIFTEEN | MILK CHOCOLATE, IF I MUST

colate,

FIFTEEN

I t's one day shy of February, and although it is the shortest month, it always feels like the longest one for a Midwesterner like me. The sun is in hiding, and the air bites like an angry dog. Come February, in these parts, you begin to believe you will never see the sun again— ever—no matter how many times you've prevailed through to spring before. Currently, I'm at my desk cocooned in a knit sweater and swaddled in my favorite FashionABLE scarf. I have a hot coffee tucked in front of my computer keys and a small mercury glass candle beyond the screen, flickering. I'm wearing fuzzy socks, and I just asked Stephen to finagle the fireplace so the room will glow and feel cozy.

Today, I had to make my space an oasis (I only wish it were the desert island kind). I was in full-force design blogger mode, doing my best to un–Pottery Barn everything and decorate for my little family when everything changed. I was going for a Scandinavia-meets-London vibe, but instead, it looked like a mix of false safety, old memories that made me sad, and uncertainty hedged in by walls and a roof. I was always divided between wanting to be at home and far from it. It seemed I craved familiarity and change equally.

I've had my days of running away and getting away— traveling to find beauty outside of my routine. Yet the thing I haven't told you is that, at some point in my running, I'm almost always abruptly reminded that, wherever I go— there I am.

The grass is never greener over there.

———— ....

This past November we traveled to Connecticut to celebrate Thanksgiving with our friends Gabe and Rebekah. I thought avoiding family holiday drama, escaping town, and being with old friends—the kind that you randomly break into dance parties with—was a really smart idea. We had a great time. We laughed a lot, stayed in our pajamas all day, watched our kids play together and put on a talent show, had meaningful conversations, ate one too many salted caramels, and had a lovely, laid-back Thanksgiving break. But I was tied up in knots before and all during Thanksgiving Day and the day after.

The knots were one thing, but there was also this guilt for

feeling wound up and bound during a time when I should be focused on all I had to be grateful for. I felt terrible for feeling this way. I tried talking myself out of it, reasoning with my emotional side. I felt like the feelings I'd tried to leave behind had caught up with me, and I hadn't actually escaped at all; I'd only brought them all with me. You see, holidays have a way of bringing out what we choose not to deal with—what we tuck away—during the other ten months of the year. The season doesn't only have to do with what's stuffed in the turkey; it has much to do with what's in us. 'Tis the season of revealing what we've been stuffing, of unveiling the great empty void waiting to be filled. I don't think anyone realized how internally anxious I was on that day of thanks, but it became apparent to me how beholden I still was to the uneasiness of a broken family.

REST IS ALWAYS AVAILABLE, EVEN IN THE MIDDLE OF RESCUE.

After goodbyes and sixteen straight hours in the car, I unpacked. Then I bulldozed my way through Christmas. I read books like *Present Over Perfect* and *Chasing Slow* while secretly wishing the whole month away—fast. I was not very present, and I favored fast. I wish I would have just remembered what I'd been learning before the holidays and what those books were affirming in me: rest is always available, even in the middle of rescue.

It's taken a few years for this truth to travel from my head to my heart. My head knew Matthew 11:30, "Come to me. Get away with me and you'll recover your life. I'll show you how to take a real rest" (MSG). But my heart did not. Bro-kenness doesn't just reveal the cracks in our hearts; it also announces the holes in our theology.

It's so easy to forget what rest feels like in the middle of hard times. We forget how to let our hair down, how to really relax. It's as if we don't allow ourselves to feel the good things because it is some sort of betrayal of the pain. When we do enjoyable activities, we aren't fully present. All of the bad senses are heightened and the good ones turned down low. I startle easy, tears flowing like a faucet, body achy, heart racing, head pounding. I feel it all. And yet I can't quite feel the cool sheets, the weightlessness in water, the arms wrapped around me. I don't really taste the chocolate.

But I'm not giving up on those small pleasures. A new fuzzy blanket. A candle that smells like my favorite store. The heat from a crackling fire. The sound of praise. Toes on a tacky yoga mat. Lingering snuggles. Milk chocolate, if I must.

I will continue to offer myself a piece of peace and open the door to the home of my heart to receive what heaven waits to give. In doing so, I'm helping myself to remember how it all feels—dialing down the volume of pain and tuning in to life's simple pleasures.

In doing so, I find my oasis.

An oasis, according to the Oxford English Dictionary, is "a fertile spot in a desert, where water is found; a pleasant or peaceful area or period in the midst of a difficult or hectic place or situation."[1]

I love to create these areas, these spots, *in the midst of.*

I've found that creating an oasis doesn't have to entail the whole house. This is where I've gotten it all wrong before. I've worked hard for my house to have a cohesive feel and look, but I've discovered that not every room invites me to relax or offers me peace. My kid's playroom, for instance: cute but chaotic. The kitchen: cozy but where so much of the work gets done. The living room: pretty but still feels formal (somehow, even with a swing).

THEREFORE, WE HAVE TO CREATE A PLEASANT, PEACEFUL AREA *IN THE MIDST OF* A DIFFICULT SITUATION OR HECTIC PLACE.

So here is what you do: pick a space where you naturally tend to exhale. I chose my bedroom, the family room, and my bathroom. Then add and subtract. I added what made the spaces feel like a retreat, a getaway, an oasis in the desert, sunshine in the winter. I set out candles that smell like coconut and sometimes aromatherapy. I brought in a fuzzy blanket for cocooning. I added logs to the fire, comfy, plump cushions, a rock-salt lamp, a footrest, and a side table to hold my tea, books, and magazines. I even indulged in a hotel-like fluffy robe and little turn-down chocolates on my bed. I continually subtracted anything that stressed me: unnecessary clutter and background TV noises, bills and paperwork, bright lights and too-tight skinny jeans.

Ideally, our homes should always be an oasis: a place of retreat, a green patch, a drink when we are dry. But that is not always the case for a number of reasons. Even in homes where all is well, there can be chaos—kids bring it through the back door every day (and I mean that in the nicest way). Therefore, we have to create a pleasant, peaceful area *in the midst of* a difficult situation or hectic place.

After a stressful day, sit in your robe, wrap yourself in your blanket, feel the heat of the crackling fire on your cheeks. Tell your mind you're turning the volume down. Allow yourself to receive rest. Rest in the rescue. It's not on the other side of your circumstances—it's right *in the midst of.* And then you won't need to wait until "this too shall pass."

Jesus said, "Keep company with me and you'll learn to live freely and lightly" (Matt. 11:30 MSG). In your oasis and outside it, keep company with Jesus. He is the unmatchable oasis—living water, a well that never runs dry. And He gives you permission to rest, Lovely One, in the middle of it all. Breathe His infallible promises and exhale your cares. He will never leave you or forsake you.

There you are; you're learning to live freely and lightly among heavy things. You are watering your own backyard, and this is where the grass is always greener—where you water it.

———— ...

The day after Christmas, I was tired of the knots in my stomach and sitting on my uncomfortable couch. Stephen and I got out the measuring tape to check, one last time, whether the couch in our basement would fit in the family room, crossing our fingers that either our room had grown or the sofa had shrunk. But again it measured "Too big! Too awkward!" We thought about it for the five minutes it took us to order a pizza for family movie night and then ran downstairs to disassemble the giant, dark-green sectional. Together we managed to carry our pretty, white couch down to the basement and bring up the "too big" sectional. It looks heavy and out of place, and it blocks our French doors to the back patio. But since we moved that couch in, we've never been happier with the room. Our whole family has found an oasis during our very long winter. Cuddling up on that couch early in the mornings with my Bible and every night watching TV together is untangling a whole lot of things in me.

Come summer, we may have to move a few things, but it's all good—we are getting good at this oasis thing.

on frie

CHAPTER SIXTEEN | ON FRIENDSHIP

dship

SIXTEEN

Make new friends, but keep the old;
Those are silver, these are gold.

—JOSEPH PARRY, "NEW FRIENDS AND OLD FRIENDS"[1]

We had matching pastel Sharp radios (with a cassette player); Ali's was mint-green, like ice cream, and mine a lilacky-lavender that any unsure-of-purple person would love. I don't remember the day we met, but I remember the radios because they somehow felt like a Best Friends necklace before there was such a thing. In those days, there were friendship pins, colored beads strung on a safety pin that you'd pass out to friends at school and pin on your Reeboks. But Ali and I had a different kind of friendship. We didn't pick each other; we didn't even go to the same school.

Our dads were friends, and by default, at four, so were we. There is something different about these kinds of friends from the ones you pick. They have a feel of family and familiarity that can never be replicated or constructed. These friends know you in your beginnings. They know the you before you became the you you think you are. They don't just know where you came from; they came from there too.

Ali moved away from the small town we lived in, and my family eventually left too. As fate would have it, the day we moved into our new home, I was pouting on the front step only to look up and see Ali playing with the girl next door. She lived a bike ride away, and this time around we chose to ride back and forth to each other's houses for sleepovers and all-day summer swims and arguing about Aqua Net ruining the ozone layer. We grew up and went our separate ways, but I've never felt like we grew apart because Ali is like family.

My children have a few friends like this. Friends they acquired as a package deal by way of their parents' friendships. Stephen and I have been vacationing with Jen and Jer since before either of us had children. Eighteen or so years later, and we are still escaping the long winters together, now with seven kids in tow.

Our friendship goes even further back. These are friends I've known since I was a girl. Friends that were once mentors (well, they still are, really) who guided me through the rough waters of being a teenager and led the way in having a living, breathing relationship with Jesus. There is history that entails mullets and breakups, concerts and retreats, and a million inside jokes along the way. They too know where I came from; they came from there too. These are old friends. These are dear friends. These friends are like family.

Spring break is approaching, and the desert house we always retreat to is not an option. Last year we rented a home in Orlando and attempted Disney World during spring break. We are not sure about this year, but the kids are adamant. (I don't deny I'm adamant too.) It's no longer just our tradition; it is theirs too. While they are different ages and there is only one girl among six boys, they've become friends, no longer just by default. They've known each other since their beginnings, and they are friends that are like family.

FRIENDSHIP CAN'T BE DEFINED BY "BEST FRIENDS FOREVER," AND IT CAN'T BE CONFINED TO ONE THING.

Last year, in a new place, with our old friends, we sat in our pajamas, laughed till we cried, and talked through the hard times life deals, the good times past, and the ones we expect in the days to come. We shared many meals, watched TV, grocery shopped together, and embarrassed our teenage kids just for the fun of it. We had only one day at the beach, which was my favorite day of the trip by far. I can't remember a day in recent years where I felt so relaxed, so at ease, so happy, so refreshed. I love the beach, but I don't think it was just the beach. It was this magical concoction of the sea, seeing my husband happy and relaxed, chilling with friends, watching all of the kids ages four to sixteen playing together at ease, seashell searching, hand-stands with Ella on the dunes, so-so seafood, and even the two-hour drive back following the wrong minivan into the wrong neighborhood.

This year on New Year's Eve we were all together, another tradition the kids have secured. They ran downstairs, and we lingered over steaks, talking about the past year—the worst part and the best. And one by one, it turned out that the trip to Florida was the highlight for each of us, for our very own individual reasons.

Sweet friendship refreshes the soul and awakens our hearts with joy, for good friends are like anointing oil that yields the fragrant incense of God's presence (Prov. 29:7 TPT). That's exactly what that day at the beach was like—the fragrant incense of God's presence.

In my adult years, I've been confused about friendships at times. I've wondered how they are supposed to look, what they are supposed to feel like. I know only what I've known or what I gather when I compare, which, of course, is only ever an assumption. One of the biggest lies I've played like a movie in my mind is that if I don't have a BFF sixth-grade style, then I don't have a real friend at all. I let myself wonder on the possibility that all my friendships are surfacey. Only I know better. They're not.

Life is no longer like the sixth grade where you call your best friend and plan to wear a matching shirt or pinky-promise to play four square at recess the next day. It's no longer about telling secrets about what boy you like or bonding over teenage angst. Now there are husbands and babies and baggage that I sometimes believe makes me a killjoy or too complicated. In this hard season, I've found my brokenness repels some and draws curious ones in, but for a few, nothing changes. It doesn't faze them; I am not my problems—they won't let me be.

Friendship can't be defined by "best friends forever," and it can't be confined to one thing.

I have many types of friends, and I'm beginning to see the beauty in that. I'm trying not to filter friendships through a mold that has been made of past friendships, hopes, hurts, or Instagram assumptions.

Today in my forty-year-old friendships, I have friends who I grab a quick coffee with, catch a late-night movie with, do yoga with, talk writing with, Vox with, take a walk with, shop with, chat on the phone with, laugh with, cry with, laugh and cry with, double-date with, decorate with, sit on the porch with—the list goes on. This is silver.

I have only a handful of friends who I share my heart with, who know me better than I know myself, who I ugly cry with, who I dream with, who I'd act like a complete fool with, who pop in unannounced and I'm OK with, who I go on trips with, who I grow with, who I would call in the middle of the night, sharing what I need help with, who could talk me into getting a tattoo or going skydiving, who I see my old lady self carrying on with. This is gold.

My friendships are all unique in their own way. The beauty is to realize the offering, whether it is a Starbucks catch-up or sharing unspoken dreams.

This past year I decided that I'm going to fixate not on having a best friend forever but rather on being the friend I want to have—forever. As in all things, it is better to give than to receive.

I found out a few years ago that the older we get, the more intentionality friendship takes. We have to seek out others who are on the same path and who have the same passions and reach out, even if it's awkward. We have to test the waters and see where they might take us. Maybe nowhere, like a stagnant pond, or maybe you'll be surfing the seas, crossing oceans of opportunity—together. I saw this happen in my life.

THIS PAST YEAR I DECIDED THAT I'M GOING TO FIXATE NOT ON HAVING A BEST FRIEND FOREVER BUT RATHER ON BEING THE FRIEND I WANT TO HAVE—FOREVER.

I want to be a friend who listens, is loyal and authentic, can make you laugh, cries with you when you cry, prays with you and for you, and is there for the big things like weddings and graduations and funerals as well as the everyday things in life like a bad-mom morning or bad haircut.

Like you, I've had friends come and friends go. Sometimes it's unintentional: someone moves and sometimes you grow apart from each other as your lives go in different directions. Sometimes, friends leave you, they betray you, they just stop being your friend. I've been there. I've felt the sting of separation and spent more time than I care to admit trying to figure out what went wrong or what I could have done. It hurts because I was vulnerable. It's hard to move on because, perhaps, I signed my letters "forever."

There is only one Friend who I know to truly be the forever kind. To be trusted always. A friend with whom your heart is always safe. Friendship is God's idea, after all. He is my best friend forever. My heart is overwhelmed that over and over again, the God of the universe calls me friend. "God-friendship is for God-worshipers; They are the ones he confides in" (Ps. 25:14 MSG). The beauty is that God confides in me.

"The amazing grace of the Master, Jesus Christ, the extravagant love of God, the intimate *friendship* of the Holy Spirit, be with all of you" (2 Cor. 13:14 MSG). The beauty is that I can have an intimate friendship with the Holy Spirit.

"God will surely do this for you, for He always does just what He says, and He is the one who invited you into this wonderful *friendship* with his Son, even Christ our Lord" (1 Cor. 1:9 TLB). The beauty is that I've been given a personal invitation to friendship with Jesus.

This is solid gold.

CHAPTER SEVENTEEN | JUMPING OUT OF AN AIRPLANE, ALMOST

g out
plane,

SEVENTEEN

"Adventure is not outside a man; it is within."

—DAVID GRAYSON, *ADVENTURES IN SOLITUDE*[1]

I t was October 2014, and I found myself strapped to the lap of a Polish man, wearing a Wonder Bread jumpsuit, at about 8,000 feet in a tiny, rickety plane with no seats. He called himself "Wonder Bob." I called myself "crazy." In this moment, I wasn't short of breath; I had completely lost it. As the plane climbed higher and higher and the landscape below became the same patchwork quilt of cornfields you see out the window of a 737 at 40,000 feet, I thought to myself, *How in the heck did I get here?*

The pilot put my hand on the yoke and said, "Here, you fly!"

"I don't want to drive!" I yelled back. Maybe it was at this point that my friend Jen knew this was not good. We held hands the whole way up. She knew me well enough to know that just stepping foot in a plane that size was no small feat. But there I was strapped to "Wonder Bob," muttering prayers, chanting Psalm 91, and attempting deep breaths, as I had been instructed to do.

We were about to skydive.

Jen locked her eyes with my blank stare and over and over chanted, "You CAN do this! You CAN do this! You CAN do this!"

"I DON'T WANT TO DO THIS!" I said with a strange contorted face, trying to hold back tears.

Wonder Bob chimed in, "I push you, OK?"

I panicked. I had a feeling that the most easily translated word in all the world, "NO," was going to be lost in translation. The door opened and I cat-crawled as far away from the open air as possible in such a tight space while attached to a strange man. "I CAN'T do this."

Jen saw that this truly was not going to happen and helped communicate to Wonder Bob that "no" means "NO!"

Jen jumped.

I sat in Wonder Bob's lap and bawled, whimpering for twenty minutes, like a puppy, like a crazy lady. The pilot circled around, giving me one last chance, and upon my refusal landed the plane. And, lucky for me, we got it all on a GoPro.

Several months earlier a few girls—Jen, Lisa, Lori, and I—met for a creative meeting for Original Conference. Over iced coffee, we were slated to discuss design and content for the upcoming conference, but in the process we ended up discussing the state of our hearts. We all knew each other, some of us friends for decades, others coworkers, all of us friendly but not accustomed to opening the deep places of our hearts. One by one, organically, we began to share our hopes, fears, and dreams. We unveiled a thread, and God was ready to weave. It was a holy moment— because something sacred happened in that space. We decided two things that day at Starbucks. One: we all needed and wanted authentic, truth-telling friendships that go deep. Two: we wanted to live intentionally, with bravery, taking actual steps toward our dreams and goals. We were ready to move past the wishing. (My friend, Jen DeWeerdt, tells this story in her book *Past the Wishing*.) That sunny day in May we formed Team Brave.

CONTINUE ON IN COURAGE BY ENCOURAGING EACH OTHER.

Two weeks later, with the addition of our friend Liz, we circled back around at Starbucks, each of us with our list of dreams and goals. We shared wishes, longings in our hearts, things we were too afraid to really go after or even give voice to (this book you're holding being one). The goals were personal, professional, and adventurous.

What would a Team *Brave* be if we didn't experience a little adventure together? And besides, all five of us, more than anything, wanted to live an adventurously expectant kind of life, greeting God with a childlike, "What's next, Papa?" (Rom. 8:15–17 MSG).

We each had our personal goals for which we would keep each other accountable, offer support, and cheer each other on. But we wanted to do a few monumental things— together—as a team. Lisa said she had always wanted to run a half marathon. Liz, too. Jen said she wanted to skydive. Lisa, too. Maybe they all did? I can't remember because I was too busy praying, under my breath, that that would not be a group experience.

Well, you already know how that turned out.

A group text went out. I can't remember who started it (probably Liz), saying, "There is a Groupon for skydiving; who's in?" Groupon + skydiving? It was a rapid-fire response, in which I stayed silent. Groupon + skydiving = dumb. An hour or so later, someone pinged, "Trina????? Why so silent?" Groupon + skydiving = dead. I don't remember my exact reply except that they all heard it as "So you're saying there's a chance?" in a very Lloyd Christmas kind of way. I eventually did say yes because, after all, I was the one at the Starbucks who shared, "Brave says yes!"

--------- ....

We went to pick up Jen from her jump. I felt the hot heat of shame. My kids didn't believe I would do it; they were right. My friends were going to be disappointed. The husbands would all laugh at me (and they did thanks to the

GoPro). Thousands would see this at the conference; I would be publicly humiliated. And worst of all, I was angry with myself. Mad because I really thought I was going to go through with it. I had said yes the best I knew how: yes each step of the way. Yes to the text. Yes to getting into the car. Yes to putting on the gear. Yes to riding in the plane.

I had pictured the moment over and over (especially when I was running for the half marathon training) like a movie trailer with dramatic music in the background that builds. I jumped. I landed. I fell to the ground and cried. Everyone cheered. And *all* fear was gone! I was pumped up and inflated on Scripture and Pinterest quotes: "Sometimes what you are most afraid of doing is the very thing that will set you free."[2] And that's what I wanted more than anything: to be free. Free from fear. Free from the torment of fear I had been fighting as far back as I can remember.

I have a lot of "almosts." I've been collecting them all my life.

01 / I almost went to Ethiopia (another story for another day).

02 / I almost spoke in front of people.

03 / I almost reached out, introduced myself, and made new friends.

04 / I almost spoke up when I had something to say or contribute.

05 / I almost took a risk.

I've missed out on a lot of beauty because of an ugly thing called fear.

Peppered in those "almosts" I have taken my share of chances, always while reciting to myself a cocktail of "Just do it afraid." "It's better to feel fear than regret." And Psalm 91.

IN THE END, THERE IS NO REAL MISSED OPPORTUNITY BECAUSE GOD WILL CONTINUE TO PLACE NEW OPPORTUNITIES IN FRONT OF YOU, GIVING YOU THE CHANCE TO SAY YES, AGAIN AND AGAIN.

I did go to Swaziland at twenty, months before I was married. I did speak in front of 2,500 women. I did travel to an out-of-state conference by myself to meet new people. I did get a tattoo. I did run that half marathon. I did make it through a medical scare. I did fight, heart and soul, for someone I love. I did stand up when someone told me to sit down.

But back on the ground the next day, more truth came out, and fragments of my soul surfaced. I spilled into my journal why I wanted to jump.

I wanted to jump for my kids to show them I was able. I wanted to jump for Stephen to show him I am fun. I wanted to jump for my family to shock them and show them I'm more than who I've always been. I wanted to jump for my friends to show them I'm not a quitter. I wanted to jump for every person who has ever underestimated me. Apparently, I wanted to jump to prove something.

After a one-day allowance of wallowing, I started to look for the lesson—because there is always a lesson. I heard a whisper, "John 2." I flipped to the story of Jesus's first miracle where He turns water into wine. I had no idea what this had to with my skydiving fail. I was thinking more along the lines of Peter getting out of the boat and then sinking. But here I was at the wedding. It was Mary's words that were for me: "Do whatever he tells you" (John 2:5 NIV).

I realized, then, what *He did not tell me*. He did not tell me, "Jump out of that airplane, Trina, and you will never be afraid again. Jump out of the airplane and prove to everyone that is the case."

I went back to Peter. Because don't we all relate to Peter? Peter said, "Yes." He took a step, but then…he sank. "Immediately," it says, "Jesus stretched out His hand and lifted him up." He lifts him before the lesson. Then He goes on to tell Peter his faith is lacking and simply asks, "Why would you let doubt win?" (Matt. 14:31 TPT).

I now ask myself two questions:

Is this something He told me to do?

Why would I let doubt win?

————————————

FEAR DOES NOT KEEP YOU SAFE.

————————————

Before skydiving, we ran the half marathon. Well, all of us but two. Lori found out early on that she couldn't run for health reasons and wouldn't even be able to attend the race. Jen was having trouble breathing a few weeks prior and decided the morning of the race that it wouldn't be prudent to run. She was heartbroken. Although it wasn't easy to sit it out, she encouraged us and cheered us on with shouts. This is what we did for each other, what we still do: we continue on in courage by encouraging each other.

Team Brave was one of the best years of my life. I lost a few toenails (three to be exact) and some pride, but I found meaningful friendships and courage in camaraderie.

My struggle with fear has taught me enough to fill a book, but in this one, I want to share a few things I've learned along the way.

01 / The only way to freedom from fear is by a revelation of God's love and receiving His perfect love. There is no fear in love (1 John 4:18 NIV).

02 / Realize that fear does not keep you safe. Susie Davis says what I have not wanted to admit in my life: "The thing about being afraid for a long time is that you start to believe fear itself keeps you safe."[3] Psalm 31:15 says, "My times are in your hands" (NIV). Over-calculating doesn't sustain life, it stifles it.

03 / Doing it afraid is better than not doing it at all.

04 / In the end, there is no real missed opportunity because God will continue to place new opportunities

in front of you, giving you the chance to say yes, again and again.

05 / There is courage in camaraderie. Do hard, scary, exhilarating, adventurous things *together*. God-dreams are never singular.

"I almosts:"

01 / ....

02 / ....

03 / ....

04 / ....

05 / ....

"I'd like to:"

01 / ....

02 / ....

03 / ....

04 / ....

05 / ....

hanging
(and hu
on mem

EIGHTEEN

"Memories aren't stored in the heart or the head or even the soul, if you ask me, but in the spaces between any given two people."

—JODI PICOULT, *VANISHING ACTS*[1]

If I told you I sometimes cry in the grocery store, would you think I'm crazy? I confess, I complain often about going to the grocery. Where I live there is no Whole Foods or Trader Joe's. I have to drive a good fifty minutes to find one, and every so often I do. Basically, I've convinced myself that if I could shop there, I wouldn't loathe it, I'd likely love it. OK, maybe that is a stretch—I'd enjoy it. I have a friend who is an executive for Whole Foods, and I asked him, "What are the chances of a Whole Foods in my town, and can you put in a word?" He didn't even let me believe for a second, like a kid with Santa. Instead, he gave me a swift "It will never happen."

I've resigned myself to the fact that I'm destined to shop at a grocery that is a very brown, supersized version of a place I vaguely recall from 1982, and this gives me mild anxiety. What can I say? Environments affect me. But between you and me, it's the music that does me in.

Bette Midler crooning "The Wind Beneath My Wings"[2] while I'm buying ground beef for tacos or talking to the deli man? *Gah!* Really? Maybe you don't even notice these songs, but it seems while I'm alone at the grocery picking out everything we need, I am isolated with my thoughts (and ground beef) and somehow, almost always through song, reminded of what money cannot buy. It overwhelms me. Christopher Cross comes on the airways, and I'm sailing through my childhood, feeling a kind of happiness that hurts; feeling old hurt that is so familiar I'm not sure how to function without it.

For a season, during my darkest days, it really did incite anxiety. I remember so clearly walking into the store and straight back out a number of times. I had to literally talk myself into walking back in because if I didn't buy groceries then, I'd have to go back with four kids in tow—and that would be worse. It felt so lonely walking the aisles with a steady flow of strangers, visiting the past, and so pathetic that the memories and the pain would betray me in such a public place. That the constitution of my heart would shove itself out my eyes and stream down my cheeks. That I had to mutter an order to my legs to move, one foot in front of the other, in the chill of the dairy aisle.

Today it was a car that pulled in front me, a champagne

Cadillac Escalade, the same one we have in Tucson. *"It's just a car, Trina!" "It's time to get over it!" "It's been long enough."* I hear in my head what others have told me, what I now tell myself. It *is* just a car. But inside the car were my mom and my dad—together—picking Stephen, the kids, and me up from the airport after a stressful flight, in which I uncomfortably nursed a baby, to spend a few weeks in the foothills as a family, making the memories that now haunt me in the produce section. Inside the back is packed with groceries from AJ's and a fancy purse my dad bought me, for no reason, from La Encantada. In the back seat, it's every one of my crying newborns, who kept me up all night crying, strapped in their carrier on the way to Sunday brunch at La Paloma—the very first place we stayed, twenty-two years ago, when the family fell in love with Tucson. In it is my grandpa Warren wearing his aviators, sitting next to Amy on the way to J.J.'s college graduation at U of A. Inside, it's the McNeillys and DeWeerdts, crammed in, on our way to one last meal at Blanco to be topped off with gianduia gelato from Frost before we all begrudgingly return to winter coats. It's not an Escalade; it's a piece of my life. It is a reminder of everything that was.

I didn't let myself go there today, although some days it doesn't feel like I have the luxury of a choice. Today I have to write. I'm on a deadline, and I can't go *there*. My heart has learned to work overtime to guard my emotions when absolutely necessary. I have to be here. That is until I'm writing this—forcing myself to listen to the music I now purposefully avoid in the grocery (by tuning in to podcasts) to feel it all, to face it. Maybe I'm making progress? I've had to leave the table only once to cry in the bathroom. Two years ago, I would have camped out in there all day.

THAT THE CONSTITUTION OF MY HEART
WOULD SHOVE ITSELF OUT MY EYES AND
STREAM DOWN MY CHEEKS.

I give myself grace for the grieving I've journeyed through, but I also give myself acceptance. I accept that I am nostalgic, that I've always been, even before there was anything to long for or return to. I accept that I am what some would call "overly sensitive" (yet, to be correct, I am a highly sensitive person[3] and so relieved to discover it is an actual thing). In the words of poet A. R. Asher, "I don't know what it's like to not have deep emotions, even when I feel nothing, I feel it completely."[4] I am compassionate, and I think and feel deeply; I choose to see it as strength. I've learned the hard way that avoiding overstimulation helps (and maybe this is why living in my childhood home has prolonged my healing process), but I cannot avoid life; it is at the grocery store and on the street. Instead I have been asking the Holy Spirit to help me. To turn down the volume on what I should not be listening to and to turn up the frequency to His kind voice. I ask Him to help me face memories. To resurface and reveal ones that need healing. The process has been a bit like looking through an old photo album or gazing at a gallery wall.

Looking at photos helps us to remember details. It brings back feelings. And, these days, I find that, many times, it reveals whether I've been idealizing the past or totally blocking it out. If we look at the past, look back as clearly, as truthfully as possible, what a teacher, mentor, and guide it can be.

HANGING UP (AND HUNG UP) ON MEMORIES | 225

"A memory can be a marvellous
getaway, but you must never
make a home there."

        -Beau Taplin

Recently, I've had to ask myself a hard question: *Could it be that I idealize the past because I fear the future? Could it be that you idealize the past because you fear the future?*

A good friend once told me, "We over-sensationalize the past. We underestimate the present. We disproportionately fear the future."

———————————

THE ONE WHO IS FAMILIAR WITH YOU,
AND WHO IS FAITHFUL, IS WAITING
FOR YOU IN TOMORROW, THE NEXT DAY,
AND EVERY DAY AFTER.

———————————

Yesterday we know, for it is familiar. Tomorrow is unknown and uncertain. But, Lovely One, the One who is familiar with you, and who is faithful, is waiting for you in tomorrow, the next day, and every day after. I don't know about you, but I long to meet Him there.

Slowly, I'm learning to fix my gaze forward rather than back. I'm making a peace treaty of sorts: that when I need to visit the past I am able to. However, it is a place I visit; it is not where I live. I don't have to get hung up there. I can hang the memories on the walls. I can see what I need to see. Listen to what I need to hear. Remember what I need to remember. Learn what it might teach me for today. "A memory can be a marvelous getaway, but you must never make a home there."[5] I hang the words of Beau Taplin on my wall too.

———————— ....

I've now listened to "Sailing," on repeat, perhaps thirty-nine times.

"...It's not far to never-never land, no reason to pretend

And if the wind is right you can find the joy of innocence again."[6]

And now I'm off to the grocery store.

Dad, Mom, J.J., Amy
Stephen, Ella, Luke, Liam Brave, and Rocco Royal:

The wind is right; we *can* find the joy of innocence again. We will always have Tucson, and we also have tomorrow.

—————— ....

How to Hang a Gallery Wall:

01 /   Pick your photographs. Choose ones that tell your story, make you laugh, make you cry (you know, the glamorous one of your grandma that will make you mist up on your way to teeth-brushing time), make you feel alive.

02 /   Decide on the look. Do you want a clean modern look of all white frames creating symmetry? Do you prefer a mismatched, playful look?

03 /   Pick out corresponding frames.

04 / Place pictures in frames and use a little Scotch tape to secure your story.

05 / Play around with arrangement options on the floor. Measure for perfection if you must; otherwise take your most central photo/frame and tack it to the wall (with a nail or 3M hook) and build around that.

06 / Don't worry about it being perfect. It won't be, but neither is the life you're displaying in it.

07 / Walk by every day and give thanks for what was.

08 / Walk by every day and give thanks for what will be.

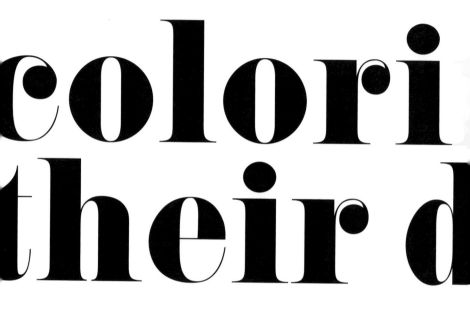

CHAPTER NINETEEN | COLORING THEIR DAYS

NINETEEN

"The landscape of one's childhood was more vibrant than any other. It didn't matter where it was or what it looked like, the sights and sounds imprinted differently from those encountered later. They became part of a person, inescapable."

—KATE MORTON, *THE SECRET KEEPER*[1]

Things I am known for: having a lot of kids, my chocolate-cherry-chip cake, La La Lovely blog, loving all things British, a deep love for God and His word, maybe a quiet strength, but assuredly for having a swing in my living room.

In my early blogging days, I visited a gorgeous old home that felt like it was from another time and place. The home was filled with sophisticated yet unpretentious antique furniture and felt as if it was plucked right out of *Pride and Prejudice*. It was fancy without being fussy. After I asked about the décor, Annie, the homeowner and designer, told me that in the Netherlands, where her family is from, children are welcome everywhere. Homes are to be used and enjoyed, which is what makes them beautiful.

When Annie shared this with me, I felt relieved. Relieved that a home could be both relaxed and beautiful. That a home could tell a story while one was being lived out within it. This is my home's destiny, I decided. It was so crystal clear. I am part Dutch, after all; decidedly it's in my blood to have a home that is lived in, used up, and bursting with unassuming beauty. And what a hued visual I had that day of my roots, which were only just beginning to be exposed.

In all its years, my house had never been stuffy, forbidding, or formal. There never was a room or a space that was shut off or off-limits to children. I wasn't raised that way. My mom let us roam freely, barefoot from backyard to basement, exploring secret storage rooms and setting up shops and clubhouses wherever we pleased. Yet somewhere in my quest to undecorate the past and redecorate with a style that I hadn't even settled into, I became a little selfish with the space. Maybe it was my attempt to get a small measure of control over the chaos that is four children. Maybe it was that I had read one too many articles about minimalism and containing toys within the confines of a playroom, as if they might contaminate all other rooms with some adolescent contagion. Maybe it was the desensitization of real life by way of Pinterest. Probably, it was all of the above.

Visiting the home that looked as if it belonged in the

center of Europe rather than the middle of Illinois and all its cornfields, I began to believe in the marriage of beautiful design and fun. I wanted a home where no room is off-limits and every room is playful and lived in. I wanted my home to be decorated with beautiful things. And most of all, I wanted my home to be festooned in imagination and colored in fun.

Even before I was a mother, I desired that my children would have memories of childhood that were nothing short of enchanting. Memories that are marked by the home they grew up in. I hoped to create a magical childhood for my brood that would help color the rest of their days.

> I HOPED TO CREATE A MAGICAL CHILDHOOD FOR MY BROOD THAT WOULD HELP COLOR THE REST OF THEIR DAYS.

For our family, it began with stories and tales and fairy explorations in the backyard. Within the home, it started with a swing suspended in the living room. And I suppose from there I just couldn't stop. If my wallet hadn't interrupted my plans, you can be assured that I would have a slide hidden in the front coat closet that would twist and twirl its way down to our basement.

Before the *Pride and Prejudice* house, there was the Chick-fil-A house: a home oozing with fun and imagination.

This house was so sticky with living; it stuck with me for nearly twenty years.

I was twenty and newly married and had just taken a job on a political campaign in Atlanta. Both politics and the South were foreign to me, but I was young and eager and grateful for the opportunity. My position was in the finance department, helping with fund-raising and chasing donations. I found that the best part of the job was coordinating fund-raisers in some of the most beautiful homes in all of Atlanta.

One Tuesday night, in the dinosaur era known as pre-iPhone-astoric, I proudly navigated my way to the southern outskirts of the city and to the home of Dan Cathy, CEO of Chick-fil-A. Most of the homes we had been fund-raising in were big, stately, and decorated to the nines, and some were, dare I say, ostentatious. This Midwestern girl had never seen so many homes so perfectly put together, so complete, so on display. But the Cathy home was different.

I remember walking through the door to find Clint, the candidate I was working for, climbing out of an enormous, sturdy old armoire. And behind him followed another person, and behind them, another and another. It was a gorgeous old piece that looked as if it was plucked from an English manor home during the World War II era.

How are people pouring out of it? I wondered. After peering into the wardrobe and discovering that it had no back and that, sadly, Narnia was not on the other side, I was told that the house had a secret staircase. The wardrobe was its entry, or escape, depending on which way you were coming or going. The owners shared what I had already assumed: that C. S. Lewis's *The Lion, the Witch, and the Wardrobe* was their inspiration.

I hadn't given much thought, at that point, to having children, but that night I decided, *When I do have children, my house will have a wardrobe that is not a wardrobe.* Who was I kidding? *I will have a wardrobe that is not a wardrobe, one that takes me to a secret place.* I confess, I don't have a wardrobe (yet), but I haven't forgotten. The home we live in is a ranch, and I can't quite find where to put a secret anything. But should we move, the wardrobe is on the top of my list.

It didn't end with the wardrobe. The secret staircase had yet another way of escape: through a bookcase that backed the walls of the dining room. Just as you'd imagine from stories you've read or old movies you've seen, an entire bookshelf slid to the right for people to sneak through a secret passageway. The dining room, which resembled a library, was outfitted in wall-to-wall and floor-to-ceiling books. And, like an embrace, they wrapped around a banquette (if I'm remembering correctly), beckoning those who dined to visit other worlds and use their imagination within the one they were in.

Not so hidden was the recognizable Chick-fil-A play-area slide within the house. It started on the second floor and coiled in circles all the way down to the basement. The home was full of fun.

At the time, I was a very homesick girl. I was missing people, of course, but also a feeling. A feeling and familiarity that I didn't have a name or language for. Yet moments upon walking through the front door I felt at home. The house was inviting, and as the night went on, I recognized pocket-sized elements that reminded me of home. A welcoming casualness that disarmed both adults and children alike. A house full of life where decorated beauty was but a backdrop. A singular coziness. Above all, I felt strangely reminded of a home that did not yet exist. I was at home in the dream of the home I wanted to build. I knew that night that wherever I made my home, I would make it magical.

> I FELT STRANGELY REMINDED OF A HOME THAT DID NOT YET EXIST. I WAS AT HOME IN THE DREAM OF THE HOME I WANTED TO BUILD.

By the end of the night, I concluded that the Cathy home was magical not by chance but on purpose. The enchanted-ness was not an accident; it was executed with thought, detail, and great care. The home fostered imagination and coddled curiosity; it had a personality I have not forgotten.

The other day, Liam, my six-year-old, called me a "Fun Sponge." Before I could let the whammy roll off me, he was so kind as to explain. He's great at details, that one. "You are a Fun Sponge, Mom, because you suck up all the fun." Clever. While he's my most perceptive and verbally adept, I knew this dig came compliments of Nickelodeon. Thank you, Nick writers. Now, I'm intellectually honest when it comes to my personality. At almost forty, I've made peace with the fact that I am not as playful as I had always perceived myself to be. I am imaginative. I am creative. And I am able to create idyllic atmospheres where fun is welcome to spontaneously combust. I just might not do the combusting. And that is OK. In accepting myself, I'm learning it is better than OK—it is good. My husband, on the other hand, is fun. I'd be surprised if he ever got dubbed a "Fun Sponge." (Well, maybe by my teenager, when he says no to Starbucks or shopping. In that situation, I am always the fun one!) However, he is not very concerned with creating atmospheres that are enchanting enough to stay with you, like your favorite story, forever. And that is OK. It is good. Because together we make a home that is fun, broken-in, enjoyed, and beautiful.

———— ....

I'm not suggesting that you have to have a swing or a slide or any playground piece in your home to make it fun, magical, or memorable. I only hope to open your eyes to the possibility of creating a home that feels like home to little ones and grown-ups alike. Let yourself imagine constructing a home so sticky with living that memories and magic dance up and down your halls and straight into your little ones' hearts.

Perhaps you are like my mom and you have no problem letting kids wander anywhere and everywhere expressing their creative freedom. Your children will remember that. They will talk about it, like my sister does to this day. Maybe you are like me and you like to design environments that are endearing. Ella already reminisces about the fairy door we had on the side of the house and the miniature gifts and notes that were exchanged. Perhaps, for you, magic is made at the kitchen stove with a little sous chef by your side. There you have fun stirring and bringing out the flavors of her imagination. Whichever way you make your home enchanted, in that effort you are sending fragrance up out of the pot, steaming straight to little noses and out into the atmosphere where one day it circles around again and invites them back home.

P.S. You should know I do have days where I wish I could block off certain rooms with yellow crime-scene tape. There are days when I yell, "Get out of the living room! It is not a playroom!" And there hangs the swing. Often, I vow to extradite all toys to the basement. But I know eventually they will make their way back up to the sunlight for us to step on, waiting to retreat to interesting hiding places, like in the refrigerator. At least once a week I tell my husband, "No kids in our bedroom. I need one room, just one room, that is kid-free." And then an hour later I let Rocco cuddle under my covers to watch *Pokémon*. Eventually, I settle myself down, sinking deep into the thought, in the same tone as my mother's voice, that soon enough my children will be grown and the house will be still and the absence of stray toys strewn across my floors just might make me homesick.

CHAPTER TWENTY | ON ACCEPTANCE

TWENTY

"Most things will be OK eventually, but not everything will be. Sometimes you'll put up a good fight and lose. Sometimes you'll hold on really hard and realize there is no choice but to let go. Acceptance is a small, quiet room."

—CHERYL STRAYED, *TINY BEAUTIFUL THINGS*[1]

I love and hate this word, "acceptance." It seems like such a buzzword these days. Acceptance, to me, holds thoughts of inclusiveness and defeat. At either end of the spectrum, acceptance always requires courage: a courage to embrace something new, a courage to let (something) go.

Acceptance has been one of my biggest struggles. I don't imagine I'm alone in this. The idea that we must accept what we cannot change feels a lot like defeat. The concept that we must accept what has changed, similarly, feels like defeat.

I've always been terrible at accepting change. Moving houses, changing schools, Becky on *Roseanne*. The trouble is that change is happening every day and in every way; so I'm reminded every time I look in the mirror. Now, I don't mind small changes or ones that say, "We just upgraded you to a suite." But life-changing change? I suck at it every time. I fight it every time.

> YOU ARE ALL OF THOSE AGES AND AGELESS AT THE SAME TIME BECAUSE, FOR YOU, TIME HAS STOPPED.

A few years into the long divorce process my family went through, I just couldn't seem to accept it. I would have "parent trapped" it if I could. Lindsay Lohan has nothing on my brother, sister, and me. I suppose, somewhere deep down, I knew it wouldn't work. That I'd be told to grow up. That I'd have to remind myself this isn't a movie. But that is the thing about your parents divorcing—it doesn't matter your age because you are *always* the child. You feel the scared seven-year-old inside you. Your inner fifteen-year-old cops major attitude. The eighteen-year-old still knows it all. You wonder if it will fix things if you do the right things, say the right things, be the good girl, just like you did at ten. Everyone wants—expects—you to go on, move on, get over it. You are thirty-something, after all. This really shouldn't affect you. But the truth is you are all of those ages and ageless at the same time because, for you, time has stopped. No, you don't have to pick a parent to live with. "You don't have be in the middle," they say. But the truth is you are more in the middle than a small child because you are in the middle of sorting out who you were as a family and who you will be.

I can't say I would call it denial. Although maybe at first there was some of that. It was that I didn't want to accept it. Like a four-year-old I crossed my arms and refused to swallow what was put in front of me. That this was truth. That this was real. That this was happening. That I could do nothing about it. That this changed so many things.

Because if I accepted it, then what?

If I accepted, it felt like defeat. What I wanted, apparently, was a fight. And that is exactly what I did for three years. I battled.

THE ONLY PERSON I HAD BEEN BATTLING WAS ME.

My grandma called one day, and between catching up and "the kids jolly well this or that," she called it out in me. "You're having a hard time just accepting this."

"Yes," I whimpered.

"I know," she said.

Not long after, I came across words that settled me: "Acceptance is not always having to do battle."[3]

I was tired. I had been holding on for so long. Finally, I realized I was fighting something I had no control over and losing myself by not letting go. The only person I had been battling was me.

Now the question became "If I continue battling, *then what?*"

The answer to that question, ironically, was not one I was willing to accept: to eventually lose myself and possibly my little family.

I uncrossed my arms. I opened my mouth. I swallowed.

First, I had to learn to accept what I could not change (which, by the way, I've had to do over and over again). Cue the Serenity Prayer that is not just for those in addiction recovery. It is for you and me.

God grant me the serenity
to accept the things I cannot change[2]
(Dear Reader, I encourage you to take a moment to read the Serenity Prayer in its entirety).

Then…I had to accept myself—at every age. You see, acceptance is accepting all of the little girls in you, wherever you left them, however you left them. At all of my ages, I found I had accepted myself based upon an identity I found in my family of origin. And without that identity, I wasn't sure of myself, even at thirty-three.

I knew I had to "Open up before GOD, keep nothing back." And He promised that:

Then..."He'll do whatever needs to be done."
Then..."He'll validate my life in the clear light of day."
Then..."He'll stamp me with approval at high noon" (Ps. 37:5–6 MSG).

I had to accept my acceptance. This kind can't be earned, worked for, or proved. This acceptance has nothing to do with what I do or don't do. It has everything to do with Whose I am. This acceptance comes by being a child of God. I accept myself based upon my identity in God's family.

ACCEPTANCE IS ACCEPTING ALL OF THE LITTLE GIRLS IN YOU, WHEREVER YOU LEFT THEM, HOWEVER YOU LEFT THEM.

These days, I'm still learning to accept myself, to be inclusive, to not exclude myself from the grace I easily give to others. I continue to accept my acceptance—this is where grieving ends and freedom begins. Acceptance, I remember, is the last stage of grief. Grieving still comes when it does, and I'm learning to accept that too, even if it is at the most inopportune time, at the grocery or on a winter's walk as it came for me today, thinking of my grandma, accepting that she is not a phone call away. The hot tears stung on my cold face, but they reminded me that I am alive and my heart is too. Today, they reminded me that she was one who taught me the beauty of acceptance.

I now know that when we come to a place of acceptance, which looks a lot like surrender, we are able to find beauty in the unknown, in the future, in the "then what?"

PART THREE

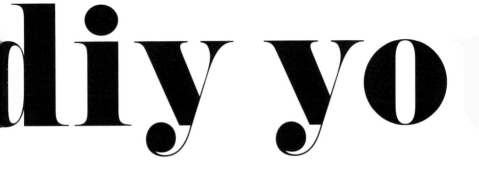

CHAPTER TWENTY-ONE | DIY YOUR LIFE

"True life is lived when tiny changes occur."

—LEO TOLSTOY[1]

C onfession: I hate DIY.

I feel lighter getting that off my chest. Even though this disclosure makes me feel like a fake. A poser. A phony.

I want to like DIY. I do. But I just don't. I feel bad about this because it is one of those "shoulds." I "should" like DIY because I'm a lifestyle blogger; it almost feels as if it "should" be a prerequisite. I "should" like DIY because it seems like the whole world does. But I don't.

I like the idea of DIY. And I like finding DIY projects to share with those who love the crafting, making, hammering, and gluing. I just don't want to do the hammering and gluing myself.

I think, for me, it all comes down to this: I'm impatient, and I don't want it to turn out wrong. I can't be bothered to wait for the paint to dry in step one before I move on to step two. And when I reach the last step ("should" I reach it), if the end result doesn't look exactly as portrayed in the photograph on Pinterest, then I failed (along with wasting time and money). Alas, there is good reason #PinterestFail is a popular hashtag.

Clearly, DIY is a craze. It's taken over the Internet, magazines, books, TV, and probably your home.

I wonder, though, if you, like me, have tried to live a DIY life? *Confession:* This is the kind of DIY I do attempt, often.

If you dabble in it, then you know the projects look different for each of us, as different as our personalities. Living a DIY life can range from *I'll do what I want, when I want* to *I don't want to do it "that" way* to *I can handle this myself* (also known as *I've got this*). Sometimes it's a deliberate choice of the will, and other times it's simply not allowing the Spirit into our everyday moments. It's hiding and hoarding our brokenness, as if it's something to be greedy with, from the only one who can do anything about it. It's trying to pay for mistakes when they've already been paid for. It's choosing to wear a weight that has been lifted, placing the chain back around our neck, like an heirloom necklace. It's hiding behind the guise of personal responsibility. Living a DIY life is trying to patch the heart and soul when we have no idea how to use spackling paste or what it even is in the first place. It's denying the mess all together. It's covering a half-patched hole with bargain art.

The thing is, *do it yourself* doesn't work spiritually. We are not meant to change things all on our own.

Confession: I love self-help books.

Let's call them personal growth or spiritual growth books. Either way, if you were to peek at my bookshelf, the books piled on my nightstand, or the ones towering on the floor next to my chair, you'd find a variety of genres: fiction, design, biographies, self-help, classics, cookbooks, and a good majority of spiritual growth. The way I read is like this: at least two personal growth books and one fiction going at the same time. I come from a long line of personal growth–loving people who buy books like they are groceries. With that thought, if books are food, I don't meal plan. I'm completely led by my hunger and find that books find me, at just the right time, through friend or acquaintance, from a link, a blog, or sometimes a random search. On my heart-healing journey, books have been like medicine, like food, like balm. I've collected so many that I've begun a shelf, a home, for these special books, these teachers, these guides, these friends, these meals for hungry hearts. I no longer see book choices as coincidence; many times I see them as divine intervention.

It just so happened that in the summer of 2014 it was my time to read a book written in 1895: *Abiding in Christ* by

Andrew Murray. My friend Christina feasts on this book yearly, like Thanksgiving dinner. I wanted a taste too. Every morning before my kids woke up, I'd sneak out to the back porch with a cup of coffee, my book, and a pen. I'd curl up on the wicker couch keeping company with an old soul who wrote from South Africa and the little birds singing their morning song. The timeworn book was bursting with new life. It was like finding treasure because within the pages I discovered the secret of abiding.

How many times had I read John 15:4–5: "I am the vine, you are the branches…Abide in Me"? Too many to count. The way I read it was that it was a work. It was my responsibility to abide in Christ. It was my work to keep myself connected and attached to the source. This book was shifting everything in me. It was lifting the weight of doing, striving, trying. It was freeing me of responsibility; trusting Him to keep me.

RECEIVING THE UNDESERVED GIFT IS WHERE THE MIRACLE OF CHANGE BEGINS.

I picked up my pen to underline: "You will learn how your best work is to listen, hear, and believe what He promises; to watch, wait, and see what He does; and then, by faith, worship, and obedience, to yield yourself to the One who works mightily in you. **One would think that no message could be more beautiful or welcome than this: that we may rest and be quiet, and that our God will work for us and in us.** And yet how far this is from being the case! How slow many are to learn that quietness is a blessing, that quietness is a strength, that quietness is the source of the highest activity—the secret of all true abiding in Christ!"[2]

Doing, striving, and trying changed to listening, hearing, believing, and yielding my botched DIY heart and life. I laid down the heavy chain that I clasped around my neck each morning.

I've often wondered why it is so hard to truly change. For hearts to be healed whole. For daughters and sons to walk in the full freedom of the Cross. I've wondered why I, over and over, take one step forward and two steps back. I've not only wondered, I've asked. Within this new wide-open space of abiding, I asked, I rested, I was quiet, and I listened. This is what I heard:

The hard work of change is receiving.

Receiving what Christ has already done for us and what He wants to do in us. It is not our work. It is His work. We tire ourselves in the trying, we wear ourselves out in our efforts to convince Jesus that we are not worthy of the gift He offers us, and we exhaust ourselves in our unbelief. It's hard to receive what seems too good to be true. New life. New beginnings. Second chance upon second chance. There must be a catch or a clause. But the truth is Jesus, and the love of the Father that He came to share, is too good, and it is true. Receiving the undeserved gift is where the miracle of change begins.

Will you allow the Father to do the work? Will you receive what Jesus has already given? Will you listen to the Spirit, our Ever-Present Help, the Divine Encourager (John 16 TPT) every step of the way? Will you rest while they work the necessary changes in the home of your heart and in your life? Will you abide?

How to not DIY your life

Step 01 / Abide. In this place, also interchangeable with remain, it looks a lot like waiting. Waiting for the paint to dry. Waiting for the phone to ring. Being still. It does a number on the impatient, on the doer and the go-getter.

Step 02 / Only revealed after step one is complete, and so each consecutive step goes. It's working with the raw materials, living in ordinary days. This is where the shift in your thinking takes place. Where you begin to notice the beauty buried in the everyday and begin to believe that ordinary moments have everything to do with your purpose and destiny. You no longer discount the ordinary moments: your waking, your mothering, your computer-key typing, your Sunday-morning serving. These are the moments you were made for. These are the moments that are making you.

Step 03 / Abide. Remain. Receive.

Step 04 / Repeat.

Confession: I don't know how it will all turn out, but it won't turn out wrong.

The finished result, surely, will not look as you pictured it. Life never does. The steps will not always make sense and may seem very out of order. Abide. Remain. Receive. If you get out of step, add a step, or skip a step, this doesn't equate to hashtag #LifeFail. If you get way out of step and relapse to DIYing, making an absolute mess out of your heart, your soul, or your life, you are never too far gone. If you still have breath, God still has something to work with. He still can free you from the care and responsibility. If someone dear to you has made a hopeless situation out of their life, as long as they still have breath, God has something to work with, and He has a thousand ways to set them free! Psalm 130:7–8 tells us to "keep hoping, keep trusting and keep waiting on the Lord; for he is tenderhearted, kind and forgiving. *He has a thousand ways to set you free!* He himself will redeem you; he will ransom you from the cruel slavery of your sins" (TPT, emphasis added).

————— ....

That summer I wrote the word "abide" on my wrist, every day, with my Pilot Precise Rollerball pen. It's a wonder I didn't get it tattooed there. I wanted to remember this new way of living, of remaining. I wanted to remind myself to stop interrupting change with my self-work, my DIYing life, and to rest and let Him do the work. It felt irresponsible to a girl whose number one strength (according to her Strength Finder's coaching) is responsibility. It still feels irresponsible at times. And if I'm really honest, these days I get more caught up in how it looks. When I stop *doing*, it may appear like I am doing nothing, like I'm going backward rather than forward. Like I'm not doing *enough*. I won't be able to pocket the accolades I'm accustomed to when I do the work myself, when I juggle the load, when I hustle, when I prove I'm responsible. But the more I abide, remain, and receive—the more of a deep change I see in myself; the more I trust that no matter how it all goes, I won't turn out wrong—the more I begin to look like the original design He has always had for me.

I'm done with my druthers.

The one who has measured the waters in the hollow of his hand. The one who with the breadth of his hand has marked off the heavens. The one who has held the dust of the earth in a basket and weighed the mountains on the scales and the hills in a balance (Isa. 40:11–12, my paraphrase from NIV) is the one who designs my life, who designs yours.

A DIY for the home to remind you to abide, remain, and receive

DIY Fringe Wall Art

Step 01 / Purchase your supplies or dig them out from your craft closet, containers, or under your bed. Here's what you will need:
+ Two brass hoops, differentiated in size. These can be found at a fabric store.
+ Colored string
+ Textured fuzzy yarn
+ Beads and embellishments

Step 02 / Place the smaller hoop within the larger one—a reminder to abide, to live in Him. "Make your home in me just as I do in you," as it says in the Message translation (John 15:4). Then tie the two hoops together, at the top, using your colored string. Secure the attachment by wrapping the string around the two hoops, over and over, where they adjoin. Read John 15 and meditate on being joined, grafted into the Vine, as you continue wrapping until the piece feels secure and you achieve the look you desire.

Step 03 / The last time you wrap the string, create about a ten- to twelve-inch tail that will wrap under and then up to be used to hang the finished piece. String beads for adorning it (like fruit on the branch) if you fancy, and then tie a knot at the top.

Step 04 / Tie yarn around the bottom of the largest hoop to create a flowing fringe (search "Yarn Wall Art" on LaLaLovelythings.com for photo instructions if you feel unsure). Get crazy. Keep it simple. Mix and match colors or keep it plain. Trim to make even or create a symmetrical pattern. Be reminded of the branches and how the Father cares for each one attached to the Vine and how He lovingly and with great attention prunes, cleanses, lifting and propping up the fruitless branches (John 15:2 TPT) when necessary.

Step 05 / Tack it to the wall and enjoy every undeserved gift.

CHAPTER TWENTY-TWO | FINDING YOUR ~~STYLE~~ SELF

TWENTY-TWO

"The most exhausting thing in life, I have
discovered, is being insincere."

—ANNE MORROW LINDBERGH, *GIFT FROM THE SEA*[1]

It seems everyone wants to find their style these days. Or at least everyone is busying themselves with some form of style-related project, whether it is themselves, their home, their blog, or their bookshelves. I really can't remember using the word "style" much in my formative years other than talking about "hairstyles." No one styled themselves or their shelves. Back then, you picked out the clothes that you liked, and you—maybe—decorated your shelves. Even at the turn of the century stylists were for the elite, for the famous. But these days it's likely your neighbor has a stylist or is one. In a world of capsule closets and stylist subscriptions that are packaged and placed on your front porch each month, it seems everyone is trying to find their style.

Only I wonder if they might just be trying to find themselves.

I've been looking for myself for a long time. Looking all over the place, really. Looking at others, and looking to others, when all along I should have been looking at myself and to God, the One who created me.

I finally figured out that to find myself, to know myself, it was best to go back to my beginnings. I don't think style is about evolving as much as it is about returning to your originality. Side note: my hairdresser once told me that your best color is the color you had when you were five (dig out your old photos and take them to your next hair appointment).

What were your earliest likings? Are there any common threads with what you seem to be drawn to today? I'm certain you'll always see early likings come out in your grown-up style.

Here are a few of mine:
+ Pretty in Pink Barbie, rainbows, and hearts
+ Mint chocolate chip ice cream
+ The Southwest and its muted colors
+ My Little Pony
+ Trinkets that remind me of travels and times I never want to forget
+ Books, for their stories and their pretty covers
+ California
+ Esprit and Benetton colored letters
+ Jeans and penny loafers

- Big dangly earrings or tiny little studs
- Sun-kissed hair and cheeks
- Newspaper print
- Dress coats and statement backpacks
- Pastel-colored everything

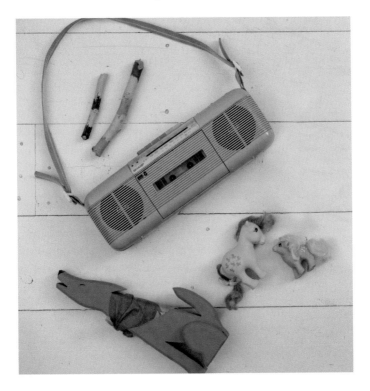

I've always been drawn to pink and mint green. When I finally got a room of my own, in the seventh grade, it was in the basement. A storage room that was used as a play-room, to be exact. My parents had it built out into a bed-room, and my mom and I decorated it together. I had a coral-colored coyote with a bandana around its neck that I had brought back as a souvenir from our family trip to Colo-rado. It became the inspiration for the look of my bedroom.

The room was complete with mint-green carpet, Southwest motif wallpaper border, and a few pieces of pottery. I loved that room in the basement with a low ceiling and no windows.

The pastel palette worked well for me in the '80s with my Southwest-styled bedroom. In the late '90s, my bridesmaids wore seafoam-green dresses, and I carried pink roses in my bouquet. In the early 2000s, I went a little silly for shabby chic. While I'd deny my wedding décor these days, here I am still picking up and drawn to dusty pinks and sea-colored greens. In fact, I recently added a gorgeous piece of cactus art to our master bedroom, and I'm only seeing the irony just now. Always evolving, always returning.

I DON'T THINK STYLE IS ABOUT EVOLVING AS MUCH AS IT IS ABOUT RETURNING.

I think broken times sometimes strip us to our starts. They peel away any pretense and bring us back to our basics. Basic needs, wants, desires, and dreams. At least they've done that for me. They've made me look back, when I was trying so hard to push myself forward. To face the little girl in me and reconcile her to the woman I am now. What was the state of the little Trina's living and lived-in home? Does it parallel or oppose the current state of my heart and home? Do we have similar needs, wants, desires, and dreams? The answer is yes. Yes, we do.

We grow out of so much in our teens and twenties. We are

herded by peers, culture, and authorities. We are told to grow up, to "be this," and to not "do that." We are eager and willing to leave our younger selves behind, and many of us do in search of a more sophisticated version of ourselves. When we reach the end of our thirties, we are no longer trying to grow up or out but into who we were always meant to become. And it's here we realize that, perhaps, we are not all there. We have left who we are behind.

IT'S LIKE THE FIRST HALF OF OUR LIVES WE PUT SO MUCH ON, ONLY TO TAKE IT OFF. WE LAYER, ONLY TO LET PIECE BY PIECE GO. MAY WE ALL REACH THE PLACE, EARLIER THAN LATER, WHERE WE ARE ABLE TO SHED WHO WE WERE NEVER WEAVED TO BE.

It's weird becoming this primal, evolved you. It's like the first half of our lives we put so much on, only to take it off. We layer, only to let piece by piece go. May we all reach the place, earlier than later, where we are able to shed who we were never weaved to be.

Me, I've always felt like this juxtaposed person who is an old soul and childlike all at once. And I am most happy being that mixed-aged person.

Beauty begets beauty. The beauty of then begets the beauty of now, and so it forever goes if you will look for it.

Your style is beautiful. So what if someone else doesn't think so? So what if it doesn't match the latest Pinterest trends? Others will revel in you being comfortable in your own skin more than an immured version of yourself trying to conform or fit in.

―――――― ....

Frankly, I'm a little astonished at the amount of pink my husband is OK with in our home. I should make a disclaimer: if you are newly married, this doesn't always work. Stephen was overly interested in the color of our juice cups when we were registering. We landed on cobalt-blue-rimmed Mexican glasses, which I would not pick out now if given the choice. (Funny thing, at World Market they are named Blue Rocco glasses. If someone would have told us that we'd have four kids and the last one would be named Rocco, I wouldn't have believed them!) I also wouldn't have picked out the forest-green floral bed-in-a-bag bedspread that we ended up with. Peppered in our picks, often influenced by others, there were a few things that I look back on and know they were true to my style: cream curtains, a comfy couch, simple white dishes.

Marriage is a new beginning, and if you marry young, like I did, it's a mixing of uncertainties and undecidedness. You still have growing up to do; you just do it together. I grew out of the blue-rimmed Rocco glasses, and we both grew more into ourselves. And you know what? It's been hard to veer from the people we fell in love with, who we were at an in-between stage of life, and fall in love with who we've always been and who we are growing into. Marriage can be a lot of "Who are you?" "Where did you go?" And, occasionally, "Oh, there you are."

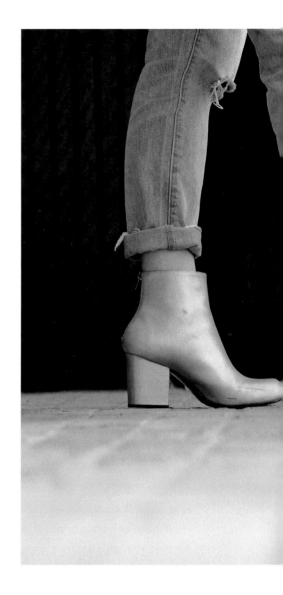

Stephen likes to hunt and is a business owner. When we married, he wore suits all the time and was a pastor. I like to write and need lots of quiet. When we married, I was more outgoing and up for anything. His home office has camo and a stuffed turkey and ram; mine has a pink wall and pretty little things. We are the classic "opposites attract," but we are opposites on the same team. After almost twenty years of marriage, we are finally learning not just to accept each other but to love each other for who we truly are, not for what we do or whom we thought the other would be.

————— ....

I wonder what God was thinking when He wove me. Was He inspired by a cotton-candy sunset with the desert mountains in the foreground when He was embroidering me from nothing to something? I picture Him scanning the movie reels of time and seeing that every thread goes with growing up in the 1980s. I picture the Father cherishing me, at every stage, every age, pleased with the masterpiece He saw long before He created.

> You formed my innermost being, shaping my deli-
> cate inside and my intricate outside, and wove them
> all together in my mother's womb. I thank You, God,
> for making me so mysteriously complex! Every-
> thing You do is marvelously breathtaking. It simply
> amazes me to think about it! How thoroughly You
> know me, Lord! You even formed every bone in
> my body when You created me in the secret place;
> carefully, skillfully shaping (embroidering) me from
> nothing to something. You saw who You created me

to be before I became me! Before I'd ever see the light of day, the number of days You planned for me were already recorded in Your book. Every single moment You are thinking of me! How precious and wonderful to consider that You cherish me constantly in Your every thought! O God, Your desires toward me are more than the grains of the shore! When I awake each morning, You're still thinking of me. (Psalm 139:13–18 TPT)

Take the time, Lovely One. Study the masterpiece you are and all of your intricacies. Give yourself permission to find yourself—then and now—and reconcile the two together. Take personality tests; take trips down memory lane and to new places you've never been. Ask the Spirit to help you remember, to peel away any pretense, and to guide you in becoming who you were weaved to be. Listen to your heart and what it beats for, and look to the One who created you. He knows all the colors He painted with and the right mix to color the gray away.

How to find your style

01 / What were your favorite colors as a kid?

02 / Where was / is your favorite place to visit?

03 / On a scale of 1 to 10, how important is comfort to you?

04 / If you were a Spice Girl, which one would you be? (Don't laugh—just answer.) I've been known to categorize my friends and family into Spice Girls.

05 / What did your childhood bedroom look like? What were your favorite things about it?

06 / What was your favorite outfit growing up?

07 / Ocean, mountains, desert, or city?

08 / Create a board on Pinterest and pin any image (people, place, food, things) that catches your eye.

09 / Meditate on Scripture that describes who you are as a child of God.

I feel like the answers to these questions should give you a number so that you can tally up a score, like in *Teen Vogue* or *Glamour* magazine. But I'm afraid that, as you already know, masterpieces can't be categorized. You are one of a kind, and so is your style.

Review your answers, observe your pins, and look for a pattern. Is there a lot of blue, pink, green? Do you see any themes? Are the images colorful or monotone? Modern or classic? Collected or minimal? Are the places exotic or calming? The best way to find your style is to notice what you return to again and again.

CHAPTER TWENTY-THREE | ON SELF-CARE

-care

TWENTY-THREE

"'What day is it?' asked Pooh.
'It's today,' squeaked Piglet.
'My favorite day,' said Pooh."

—A. A. MILNE, *WINNIE-THE-POOH*

M y mom says there are two times a year that are the hardest for a mother: the end of winter when everyone gets sick and you are waiting for spring to come and the end of summer when you are ready for school to start.

She is right, as always. It's February. I'm convinced the only people who like February are those who have birthdays, anniversaries, or some kind of special day tucked between the first and the twenty-eighth and those who live in California. It is the shortest month of the year, and yet it always feels like the heaviest. The days just kind of sit on you, weighty, like a child too big for carrying. They feel like they have skipped out of the rhythm of sunup to sundown and have bookended themselves from foggy to dark. The air is cold, and the wonder of winter has departed, leaving behind a muddied mountain of snow in the mall parking lot. February is when I daydream about the beach, the Catalina Mountains, anywhere but here. You too? It's twenty-eight days of living in the marrow of winter.

This past week we were in the throes of February. Rocco was recovering from a cold, which I caught. I gave myself one day to rest, which felt like a luxury, especially because I watched an hour of Netflix while the kids were at school. The next day, still not feeling great, I got back to writing, and by lunchtime the school nurse called saying Liam had a fever. I wasn't that surprised; he did say his throat hurt a little before he left that morning. A visit to the walk-in clinic confirmed it was strep throat. As a card-carrying germaphobe, I did my best to quarantine, Lysol, and sterilize, but the strep was stronger, and a day later Luke had a fever and Stephen caught the cold. We were quite a sight with sheets draped over sofas, Kleenex crumpled everywhere, and meltdowns over Mucinex. The majority of the week was spent measuring medicine, overdosing on TV (will I ever get the Jessie theme song, "Hey Jessie," now sung as "Hey Jet ski," out of my head?), iPads, and popsicles. To top things off, we could no longer go to our beloved pediatrician because of our insurance. And when I went to the walk-in (with four children, two separate times), I was told our health insurance was inactive—read: we were not covered. My normal response to all of this would have been a complete meltdown. As in, freak out in the junior high kind of way with whining and tears and tantrums until the only thing left to do is retreat to your room until you reemerge to pretend like nothing ever happened.

But something happens when almost everything feels out of control in your life: you realize nothing was ever in your control in the first place, that you've been scraping to hold on to ephemeral moments rather than lifelong and eternal ones. Maybe it's just that I'm realizing I've lived in one too many days that were not today. I've taken up worrying about problems, trials, and tribulations like a hobby, like it's some form of self-care.

SOMETHING HAPPENS WHEN ALMOST EVERYTHING FEELS OUT OF CONTROL IN YOUR LIFE: YOU REALIZE NOTHING WAS EVER IN YOUR CONTROL IN THE FIRST PLACE.

This past year I've added self-care to my job description, right after wife, mother, daughter. I've always thought self-care to be important. I bought the line, some time ago, that "we must take care of ourselves so we can take care of others." I wrote a blog stating that we must be kind to ourselves…so we can be kind to each other, listing ways I was going to start being kind to myself: feed my soul daily, LOL and then repeat, move my body every day, pamper myself in practical ways (wash my face, take a bath—necessary luxuries). I bought it all; I just never wore it. I wrapped myself in the stress, anxiety, worry, and brokenness of my life so tightly that it came out in my body. Self-care, the true version, was no longer just a good idea; it was a necessity for my health.

I'd take a bath bubbled up in guilt. I'd shut my door and do yoga, feeling tight for the time I was taking. I'd go on a walk and take frustration along for being so needy. This also is not self-care. It's self-sabotage. If you are doing the act of care but not caring for yourself in the process, you are only wasting time. Guilt, tension, and frustration cannot be participants. Whether you invite them to come along or someone sends them with you, you must refuse their company.

In December, during the wonder of winter, we had a glorious snowstorm. I love snowstorms because they are like God has whispered, "HUSHHHHH," blowing kisses of snowflakes to cover the earth in quiet. This snowstorm, however, wasn't quiet. It was loud. My husband plowed for forty-eight hours straight, there was Christmas shopping and baking to do, and the temperatures were too cold for the kids to go out and have snowball fights. So I did what any housebound mom would do. I made the kids lunch and put a movie on. I then drew a bath and locked myself in the bathroom with a book, a little salami-and-cheese plate, and a soothing drink. The kids banged on the door, and so did guilt. I didn't let them in. (Don't worry, my children are old enough to be on their own in another room.)

I'VE LIVED IN ONE TOO MANY DAYS THAT WERE NOT TODAY.

Apparently, it's taken me fourteen years of parenting, unraveling, uprooting, and writing a book to really begin to

live in the everyday. To look past the Kleenex, amoxicillin, and everyday inconveniences as a curse and to instead see it all as a blessing, as beauty. It's the test I keep retaking, and I think I'm finally getting the lesson.

Self-care was an escape—to the bath, to the movies, to the store, to Starbucks, back to my writing. However, accepting the day rather than fighting it (there it is again—acceptance) is a new way to be kind to myself. I still think a bath at the end of a day or dispensing medicine while not feeling great myself is a good idea, but focusing on what went wrong or did not get done is not. Yesterday, I had everyone take a nap. While they did, I watched a cheesy British mystery with tea and chocolate. And the best part is, I then had the energy (although let's just call it what it is: the grace) to be able to put together a dinosaur puzzle and to fill up more spoonfuls of the pink healing drink. You see, there is grace for today and still enough for tomorrow and every day and every deadline after that.

ACCEPTING THE DAY RATHER THAN FIGHTING IT IS A NEW WAY TO BE KIND TO MYSELF.

It's Monday. The kids all went back to school. Although I think Ella has now caught the cold. I'm behind in my work and tired, but today is not sitting on me. I feel light for the letting go, for the beauty I've seen in the color of the popsicles I passed out all week.

My Self-care routine

01 / Find a moment in the middle of crazy. Find a color that catches your eye. Notice the shape of your child's smile, the deep blue in their crying eyes, the sweet slant on their nose that you never noticed.

02 / Do something for yourself every day. Try to decide what it will be and when at the beginning of the day or the night before so that you have this to look forward to. Take a walk. Take a bath. Take time to call (not text) a friend. This kind of taking is a good thing.

03 / Light a candle and play soothing music while you work.

04 / Skip a load of laundry while the baby sleeps, and lie down, read a book, watch a show (I never followed this advice, and I wish I would have).

05 / Ask for what you need. If you feel at the end of your rope, tell your husband, your mom, or a friend. Ask them to give you a few hours to rest or retreat.

06 / Epsom salts, a good moisturizer, and eye masks (the sticky little half-circle ones from the drugstore) do wonders.

07 / Read a book for entertainment, not for education.

08 / Exercise. Who wants to do that when you are tired? But it helps, almost always. I've found running, walking, Pilates, and yoga are just as good for my mind as they are for my body.

09 / Stop and give yourself a breathing break. I find I hold my breath, especially when I'm stressed. Take five minutes to close your eyes and take deep inhales and exhales.

10 / Tell guilt bye-bye. Like, literally out loud, if you must (I must most days).

CHAPTER TWENTY-FOUR | HEAVEN KNOWS

"I want to be thoroughly used up when I die."

—GEORGE BERNARD SHAW[1]

H eaven knew we needed each other.

In the 1980s and the here and now.

"Remember that time you came to visit?" my grandma asked me several years ago.

I did. It was the summer after fourth grade, and my parents put me on a plane to Colorado Springs to visit my grandma. Some things you never forget: like flying on your own, for the first time, at age ten. I remember we went, in her blue Volvo, to the mall and up the mountain, near NORAD, to the zoo. We ate cheese toast while she watched *Murder She Wrote* and I played store in her basement. At some point during the trip, I went out for pizza for my cousin Ben's birthday and never went back to my grandma's. I don't recall any kind of handoff; I only remember playing store with my cousins and going to the Garden of the Gods. Twenty-some years later, my grandma told me the story in full and the part I never knew I played. While we were admiring magnificent rock structures, towering high above us, she was at a rock bottom. Alcoholism had brought her to what she thought was the end. But because of this little life, her own flesh and blood, at her side, in her home, she reached out for help—this became her beginning.

Heaven knew she needed me then.

We've always had a special bond, she and I. From the time I was little, my mom would point out things I did just like my grandma. I never learned these traits since we lived in separate states. They were inherent: mannerisms, postures, talking with my eyes closed, hyperextending my fingers, how I held my head. As I grew and we got to know each other, we found our similarities went beyond the exteriors.

In my late teens, Grandma Hilda would come to town to visit, and she would take each grandchild out to eat. She'd let us pick the place. With piping-hot coffee in hand, she would ask all the right questions and listen, in a most active and intent way (one of her most admirable qualities). And then in a perfect kind of timing and a most unpresumptuous way, she would spill wisdom. Pour it out like water from a pitcher. It was around this time when I realized that she was not just my grandma…she was a wise woman.

I thought this wisdom came from the millions of books she read. The ones she marked up in red (the same way my dad marks up his books and I mark up mine). I also thought that her wisdom was a God-given gift. I thought right. But what I didn't find out until many years later was that her wisdom came by way of brokenness. By not staying in a fragmented, crippling place but by living a life of surrender and letting the Lord lead her out.

The last twenty-nine years of my grandma's life were devoted to serving God by ministering to women in recovery. In my growing years, I always remember her talking about "her ladies." Only I had no idea who these "ladies" were. I figured it was a church Bible study or something of the sort. She had always made it sound so important and so official. Only now do I see how important and official it was. It was her life's calling, and it was God's official business.

She always had teaching in her. As a young lady, she  received a degree from the Royal Conservatory in Toronto and later used that degree to teach piano. During World War II, my grandma took a job as a reporter at the local newspaper, *The Edmonton Bulletin*, where she was endearingly called "Jeep" because she was small and fast. This is where she met my grandfather and what began the start of a long career in the newspaper business for her and my family.

The last few years of my grandma's life she wasn't able to do all that she was accustomed to doing. She wasn't able to meet with her ladies any longer, and I think that only aged her more. She had always been a person who found purpose in her work and worked out her passion.

Around the same time, in my life everything had come to a full stop while I dealt with a terrible allergic reaction and liver injury while still in the throes of brokenness.

Heaven knew I needed her then.

We'd talk, every now and then, and whenever we did, she'd pour out wisdom, and I'd lap it up. I'd grab my journal and write down exactly what she said. On the occasions when we were together, I'd sometimes record her talking. And before I knew it, she began sending me books. (Well, my aunt did the sending, to be exact. Thank you, Aunt Pat!) One package after another filled with books that were guides through her brokenness: the books that she then used to lead her ladies.

THROUGH THE LINES ON HER FACE AND IN HER FRAILTY, I SAW THAT BEAUTY IS NOT LOST WITH AGE; IT IS AMPLIFIED. THOUGH NOT EVERYONE RECOGNIZES IT OR RECEIVES ITS VALUE.

The packages were always followed by a scheduled phone call, where she would ask questions and then assess.

Sometimes we would just catch up, but more times than not there was an agenda. Every conversation was a heavenly download. I can still hear her proper, solid, slightly sounding like the Queen, sure voice: "You see…" "They jolly well know…" "I go back to the Word…"

During one of our calls, I remember her telling me she was so ready to go to heaven, after doing an extensive study on the place. She said she had been asking God why she was still here and felt as if He told her it was for her family. She realized I needed her, along with others in her life, and that her work could continue with us.

Through the lines on her face and in her frailty, I saw that beauty is not lost with age; it is amplified. Though not everyone recognizes it or receives its value.

One of the most important things she has ever said to me was off the cuff on one of our calls: "God is the easiest person to please." I can hear her emphasis, her pronunciation, and the hint of her Canadian accent.

"God is the easiest person to please" has untangled so much in me. The words unlaced the tight knot of perfectionism, people-pleasing, and performing. The tie that began to tangle as a little girl when I somehow sub-consciously cued into the pattern that if I behaved a certain way, if I performed, if I was pleasing to my parents, teachers, friends, and church leaders, I would be noticed, well liked, loved. Because this worked with people, I believed this was how it worked with God, times a thousand million. I believed there were strings attached. And so I tangled myself up in them. This knot, I learned, also had to be undone in her.

"GOD IS THE EASIEST PERSON TO PLEASE."

I assumed "God is the easiest person to please" was her idiom, her own guided gumption. I know she had lived out the lesson; it looks like David did also: "When someone turns to you, they discover how easy you are to please—so faithful and true!" (Ps. 25:8 TPT).

She left me with many words that I'm still working through, but the other words that took deep root and are rightly wrapping around me are: "Obey God and leave the conse-quences to Him."

I couldn't begin to tell you the balm and the beauty that I found in her stories, her life lived—filled with pain and heartbreak often masked with glamour and success—her wisdom, her teaching, her listening ear. But as we contin-ued to talk regularly and send books and notes back and forth, it turns out she, too, was finding beauty. She was find-ing it in sharing her broken years. To release them from her soul and let them take sail to help steer the future of those right behind her.

Heaven offers us each other. Heaven knows whom we need.

In the same way Jesus was sent as hope in the flesh, the Father is still using flesh to dispense the message of hope. Hope is dealt through the older to the younger and the young to the old. From the weak to the strong and the strong to the weak. Sometimes we don't even realize the hope we carry because it is disguised by hurt. Healed hurt is never to be kept to ourselves. Our healed hurt is another person's hope. Your story is the vehicle.

HEAVEN OFFERS US EACH OTHER.
HEAVEN KNOWS WHOM WE NEED.

What if we made it our job, young or old, to distribute hope?

Today it's been six months, to the day, since my grandma passed away.

I was at the K4 gate at O'Hare, in the American Terminal, the *Home Alone* one that always reminds me of my family vacations, across from the food court, in line to board a plane to Denver. I had bought a plane ticket the night before, and I thought I could make it to her to hold her hand, the same shape and size as mine, one last time. But as I was lining up to board the plane, my sister called to tell me she was gone. Just like that, gone. Here one moment, and heaven the next. I curled up behind my carry-on suitcase, tucked in a corner by the window, and sobbed for more than an hour until my mom came and collected me.

Heaven needed her.

It's been six months since my grandma left us. I don't like to think of her as gone, really, because I feel her all the time. When I have a piping-hot cup of coffee between my hands, the aroma and the warmth are like one of her signature hugs, where she would draw me in to get a good look, rock me side to side, and say, "Ohhhhhhh!" And while her arms still held me, she would recite over and over like a broken record, "Look at you, look at you," with a bob from side to side, as if she was seeing me for the very first time. On my very last visit with her, she added on a "Have I died? Am I in heaven? Are you really here?" Whomever she was with, she always made them feel like the most important person to her. I certainly did.

A few years ago, when I was visiting my grandma, standing in her galley kitchen that faced the Rocky Mountains, I asked her if I could share her story should I ever write a book. Without hesitation or reservation, she said, "Yes!" On the last visit I had with her, I told her that I was working on a book, that publishers were looking at my proposal. Only I never was able to tell her that it happened. It was on my birthday that I found out a publisher was interested in my book, and it was on her birthday that I received the offer. Call it a coincidence, if you will. I call it a God kiss. It was my dream to dedicate a book to her. To have her hold in her hands a bound sliver of her story. A story that is still being written because I am her story and my children are her story. The broken pieces of her heart were never discarded.

No, the rubble of past lives is always used to build anew (Isa. 58 MSG). I'm rebuilding with her ancient ruins.

Although she was ninety-two, I thought there was time. I was keeping the secret to share it in person. I wanted my news to be followed by a "Look at you, look at you!" Even as I was rushing to the airport to get to her, to say goodbye, to say "I'll see you on the other side," I had hoped I could whisper it in her ear. That she would know before she had to go. Of course I wanted her to be proud of me, but it was more than that. She was in a bad way. What I really wanted her to know was that her work was continuing. That sharing hope to broken ladies will go on and on.

When I finally made it back home from the airport that day, my cousin Jessica told me how she was sitting with grandma, holding her hand. She said she had told her earlier that day or maybe the night before that I was coming. My aunt and uncle were reading her some of her favorite Scriptures, singing some of her favorite hymns. My sister was singing over her: "Jesus is here and angels too." Right before her new beginning, Jessica told her that she didn't have to wait or keep holding on. She told Grandma not to wait for anyone else and that God would take care of her family. She trusted us all to God and let go. Maybe our whole lives God is asking us, preparing us, to trust Him and to learn to let go for that very moment.

I see her now as a guiding star more than ever (thank you, Erin, for that visual). I hear her wisdom reverberate in my soul; I know it's etched in the fabric of my heart (like it says in Prov. 6:20–22). I see her petite hands, with a slight slant and a bend at the knuckle, every time I look down at my own. They've always felt like they were carbon copies or maybe on loan. She played piano keys, and I type on the computer. I'll also use these hands to pass out hope to carry on her work. Her love of wisdom lives on through the red-pen underlines in the many books she sent me and the ones I now mark up on my own. Most of all I am surrounded by her in that great cloud of witness watching over me. I haven't studied heaven much—but guess who did? My Grandma Hilda. She said, "Why would I not research where I am going? I always prepare for a trip."

On Thanksgiving, I was in my friend Gabe's study, taking a phone call and nosing through his books. I took one off the shelf on the subject of heaven and began to read that those who have gone before us are still actively praying for us—with direct access to the Father. Wouldn't you know, it was my grandma's study book of choice, *Heaven* by Randy Alcorn.

I made a promise to her to continue her work. Although it might not look exactly the same, I will be seeking out the broken and sharing hope. The last time we spoke, she couldn't speak. It was mumbles, which only my dear aunt could interpret. Grandma wanted to know if I received her latest package and that I was OK. And I wanted her to know, again, that I would continue her work. I would love and obey God always, I would love my family because there is nothing more important than that, and I would share hope. This was her legacy.

I have a hard time believing that her work with me was done. Some days I contend with God about this. About more loss. About His timing. I don't feel strong enough, sure enough, ready enough. My feet are wobbly, my soul still searching. But I'm letting the Holy Spirit teach me. He was her teacher, after all. Hand in hand we are finding ways to hand out hope.

Jeep is small and again fast. She leans over the balcony with her notepad to get the scoop. She is still playing an active role in my life, keeping watch and cheering me on. She's still at work about the family's business as she has always been, only now she is reporting directly to the Father.

Heaven needed someone on that beat.

———— ....

Who in your life can offer you wisdom of years or a safe place, speak hope into your life, and show you beauty in the most unexpected places? There is beauty and wisdom and love in grandparents and the older generation that can be found nowhere else.

Do you still have a grandparent?

01 /   If your answer is yes, I must tell you: you have treasure. Maybe you just don't yet realize it.

02 /   Ask questions. Listen to stories. Receive wisdom.

03 /   Have you looked at spending time with the elderly as cumbersome (I did when I was younger)? I'd give anything to listen to my grandpa talk for an hour about his flight pattern on his plane simulator. It was always hard to pay attention when the little ones were tugging on my legs, but I did my best to listen because I had great regret for rushing my Grandma Eleanor off the phone so many times.

04 /   Grandparents are the best prayer warriors. All my grandparents are in heaven, but I've adopted Memaw, my husband's grandma, as my own. And if I need someone to pray—she's one of the first to call.

CHAPTER TWENTY-FIVE | THE SOUL OF A HOME

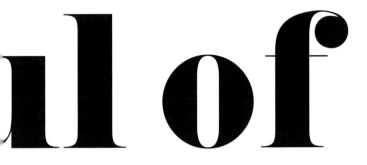

TWENTY-FIVE

*"The house, she'd explained to them many times,
had spoken to her; she'd listened, and it turned out
they'd understood one another very well indeed."*

—KATE MORTON, *THE SECRET KEEPER*[1]

I'm eight, maybe nine. With a sleeping bag under my arm (a blue one with a blonde girl holding up an umbrella to shield herself from a shower of rainbow hearts), I wiggle out of the station wagon and say goodbye to my mom. As I walk up to the front door, I start to feel sick. I can't decipher if the bubbled-up excitement I felt all day at school is really excitement after all. Because if it is, then it is the same feeling as being nervous. After kissing my mom goodbye, it's all good and games and Keebler Elf Cookies until it's time to go to bed. Suddenly it's "lights out," and I want to say "peace out" (only we didn't say that back then) and run out the front door. It's strange because

I'm positive over playing foursquare at recess I wanted to sleep over. Now, in the night, I'm not so sure. My stomach is telling me that I made a big mistake. Something is not right because nothing is like my house. Not only do I want to go home, I wish I had never said yes in the first place. I want to call my mom. But I don't want to ask to use the phone. (Do you remember this feeling? Lucky kids today with their cell phones.) It's not that I got into a fight with my friend; it's simply that everything feels different. I want to go home. There are animal heads on the walls staring at me, and what if we have eggs for breakfast? I hate eggs. And I've been taught to eat what is put in front of me and to never offend the cook. (I remind myself this also means never to ask for ketchup with my steak.) It's like I've left my planet for a night and I'm making my home on someone else's.

The cosmos is off. I am out of place.

Do you remember that feeling? I do. It stays with you, somewhere down in the deep places. My sister and I talk about that feeling and how it doesn't flee when you are an adult. How it is fully possible, as a grown girl, to end up somewhere only to find your excitement contorting into that wonted pit in your stomach. Your heart begins to beat fast, you are sure sleep will elude you, and then, one foot in front of the other, you begin to follow the trail of thoughts that ignite like a wildfire: *This was a bad idea! Why did I think this would be fun? I should have stayed home! I don't want to tell anyone I need to leave.* If only calling Mom and having her come get you could fix everything. Even if she could just get you out of eating eggs for breakfast, that would do.

Homes have personality, you know. Your childhood home. Your friend's house. The home you are raising your children in. It doesn't come by way of decorating and redecorating, by creating or changing a look. Rather, I'm convinced it's a feeling.

Don't misunderstand me, as it may appear, throughout other parts of this book, that I contradict myself—telling you that changing exteriors can have an effect on the interior of your life. I believe it can. I believe it is all connected. In the same way caring for our bodies is caring for our souls, caring for our souls *is* caring for our bodies. It's both complicated and simple. You see, a constructed cozy environment is merely a visual invitation to accept what it is offering: comfort and rest. I'm big on the visuals because they tell the story, set the stage, make the atmosphere. They are what take us back to the feeling. I find I like to create or change a look because, many times, it is a representation of the feeling I want to create or let go of. Other times it is simply a manifestation of what is. In the end, should you accept the constructed cozy environment's invitation to rest, I bet the feeling you experience will go beyond comfort and rest and may best be described as "togetherness."

Somewhere along the way, when I was little, around the time of the sleeping bag and the sleepover, I began to believe that my house had its own unique feeling—the soul of a home.

My house has history, a museum of memories. It is mine now; it was my parents' long before. And before us, there was *them*, the original owners who built the house in 1976. The house was crafted in a rather basic way on the outside with brown siding and brick adornment. Yet on the inside, and beyond the back gate, the design told tales of travels abroad.

The house was designed to be sophisticated, but it had a different kind of soul. I knew it at age nine.

As of 1986, its story had really just begun. Its starts were exotic, colored in blues and red and black inspired by other lands. But where it went from there could only be determined by whom it took in. The walls held wallpaper along with rich stories of trips to the Orient. At first glance, my young eyes found the place intriguing and imaginative. But my old soul felt that, maybe, what the house really wanted was a family to call it its own. Its walls wanted to hold homework and smudge marks and twenty different shades of paint. They no longer wanted to tell stories that were lived in faraway places. No, they wanted life lived within. It was as if the walls invited us to live our stories between them. The unassuming 1976 brown ranch, with a little bit of brick, wanted childhood and adolescence; it believed it could absorb all of the growing pains. The house wanted to become a home.

And that is exactly what happened in the summer of 1986. With the Bangles, Bananarama, or maybe Billy Ocean playing on the radio, we showed up in a moving van full of hope, with all of our toys and troubles, to the house that became a grandpa-person of a home where we all belonged.

———— ....

"Gezellig [heh-SELL-ick]," the Dutch say.

"Hygge [HOO-guh]," say the Danish.

These words have been traveling repeatedly from Europe to our screens and magazines over the past few years, with no direct translation in English. Both words from both languages are most closely translated to "cozy." Though any Dane or Dutch person would tell you the words mean so much more.

I translate them to mean: *The soul of a home.*

The Dutch may expound on Gezellig as a mood or a feeling. A nice atmosphere or a pleasant experience. Some even say it is the heart of Dutch culture. It's a quaint café with friends. It's a home that is cozy, warm, and inviting. It's togetherness and belonging. A place can be Gezellig, and so can a person.[2] Ahh, a living and lived-in home—Gezellig.

Could it be that we are all searching for a something that doesn't have a translation?

It isn't any wonder to me that "hygge" was up for Oxford Dictionaries' 2016 "Word of the Year." Oxford defines hygge as "a quality of cosiness and comfortable conviviality that engenders a feeling of contentment or well-being." And most interestingly, "[i]t derives from a sixteenth-century Norwegian term, *hugga*, meaning 'to comfort' or 'to console,' which is related to the English word 'hug.' Associated with relaxation, indulgence, and gratitude, *hygge* has long been considered a part of the Danish national character."[3]

I'm stuck on these words. Not because they are trendy. Quite the opposite, really. Because of their history. The national togetherness of whole countries, for centuries, preserving cozy, warm atmospheres of togetherness and a way of life for their people.

I'M ESTABLISHING THE CULTURE AND THE CHARACTER OF MY HOME AND ITS PEOPLE. "TOGETHERNESS" HAS POTENTIAL TO CARRY ON FOR GENERATIONS. AND WHAT I DESIRE MOST IS THAT MY HOME, LIVED IN AND LIVING, IS NOTHING SHORT OF A COMFORTING HUG.

It might not be the culture of my country; however, I translate it like this: I'm establishing the culture and the character of my home and its people. "Togetherness" has potential to carry on for generations. And what I desire most is that my home, lived in and living, is nothing short of a comforting hug.

Does your home have a feeling?

What kind of soul do you want your home to have?

Of course, it can happen accidentally, and I even dare say it will. But Dear Reader, why not be intentional about it? Why not set intention into the feeling and soul of your home?

I want the soul of my home to be restful, relaxed, creative, and fun. Stephen would argue that our house is anything but peaceful. It feels wild most days with four children, three of

gezellig

them boys. It is loud, and there is wrestling and yelling, sibling fights and snacks crunching underfoot. Sometimes (OK, most days) I yell over the kids to get their attention (even though I swore I'd never be a yeller). It's crazy in our house, but in the midst of crazy, there is love. I believe it, so much so that I bought a piece of art that reads, "IN THE MADNESS THERE IS LOVE," and hung it right in the thick of it, between our kitchen and family room. I've had to change my tune from "where there is quiet and calm there is rest and peace" to "where there is love there is rest and peace." And then what we lack in calm I try to make up for in styling the sofa with blankets and cushions, a soft place to land, just beyond the WWE ring. Each night with deep inhales and breathy exhales we tell Hulk Hogan, Dusty Rhodes, and the Ultimate Warrior to go to bed. And then we rinse and repeat.

THE SOUL OF A HOME ISN'T DETERMINED BY HOW IT IS DECORATED; IT IS DETERMINED BY WHO AND WHAT RESIDES IN IT.

This house, ever since I've known it, has been a place where you can kick off your shoes and stay awhile. Sink into the sofa and settle into your favorite show. Retreat from the world and its assaults. A little realm of rest, open to guests and family and friends and occasionally to ones who needed a temporary home.

Growing up, I recall overhearing visitors, on more than one occasion, tell my mom how there was something about our house. That it was welcoming and so peaceful. I felt it too. But clearly I knew it wasn't always peaceful. There was fighting. There was yelling. There was WWE wrestling and dysfunction. But God was there. Not just in word but in practice. His love was central. Bibles open, prayers in our atmosphere. It was not in ritual but in relationship. Looking back, I believe it was because of the practice and the prayers that there was a peace. This, I think, is what is called "a peace that passes understanding." A lack of fighting did not usher in the peace. There was peace in spite of it. It passed over and through our understanding in such a way that its presence took up residence with us.

In this new era, my second time around, Stephen and I have brought in things like creativity, quality time around the table, an addendum to fun, and many other dynamics including our own dysfunction (because don't we all have it?), but at its core I still believe the soul of this home is peace, rest, and retreat. The gezellig is still going strong.

The soul of a home isn't determined by how it is decorated; it is determined by who and what resides in it. Should we ever move, I'd grieve the house like a grandparent I can't bear to say goodbye to. But perhaps, like a grandparent gone, the good follows you all the days of your life. Perhaps you bring the feeling, the gezellig, with you as you create and grow new and unique characteristics. If ever new walls take us in, I've settled it that I will always bring with me peace, rest, and retreat. There will be prayers going up, the Word spread out, and praise dancing down the halls. God's love will be central, and peace will pass over and through our understanding and take up residence with us.

And wherever we live, we will be home.

the sto
your s

CHAPTER TWENTY-SIX | THE STORY ON YOUR SHELVES

ry on
helves

TWENTY-SIX

*"My mission in life is not to merely survive but to thrive;
and to do so with some passion, some compassion,
some humor, some style."*

—MAYA ANGELOU[1]

T here are those who fill their bookshelves with only books, and there are those who decorate their shelves with objects. And then there are a handful of us who fall into both categories. The bookshelf in my bedroom is spilling over with books (literally onto my floor) stacked, sorted, and situated for accessibility. In our family room, however, the shelves are styled with objects, trinkets, memories, pottery, and a variety of pretty little things, which happen to include groupings of books turned backward. (I know, I know. It was a trend that hit the lifestyle blogging community ages ago, and I'm still a fan.)

Either way you look at it, shelves, as far as I can tell, are for holding stories—those we escape to and those we return to. Stories we are trying to create for ourselves or the trajectory we are trying to change. The stories we have lived and want to visually remember.

If you were to invite me over, you'd probably find me meandering toward your shelves. I'm drawn to them like a magnet. Don't worry, it wouldn't be to gauge whether you know how to style a shelf. I adore looking through others' book collections because I want to read their story. It tells me about the person's interests, what they've been through and what they are working toward. And just as much, I adore admiring and contemplating shelves stacked with trinkets from trips, art, and photographs. The best homes are ones that are like private museums. Not because they are old or stuffy, rather because they are living exhibitions, curated menageries, of lives lived.

If you studied the shelves in the home of your heart, what kind of collection would you find? What stories would your shelves bear?

I sometimes forget that I can trade out what sits on my shelves. I style them and then leave the look for years. I believe it is the same in our "living home." We grow accustomed to what is situated on our shelves, even if what we have been collecting is ill-fitting. Lived in or living, either way, it takes work to change.

Yet we have the ability to change the accessories in our lives. The things that no longer serve us, tell the story of who we are, or leave no room for beauty can be exchanged. Perhaps we just need to be reminded that we are not stuck with what we picked up along the way or what others have picked out for us or put upon our shelves.

I'm thinking lately about what I display.

Fear, repeatedly, tries to situate itself, like an old earned badge front and center. And there it stays until I trade it out for love. It works its way back, again and again, like it owns a spot.

Trina, you don't have anything to say that hasn't already been said. Why would anyone care to listen to what you have to say? Don't speak up. In fact…be quiet.

Trina, if you take that risk, if you say yes, something bad could happen. Trina, what if "this"? What if "that"? What if it all falls apart?…What if? What if?

"What if" is engraved upon the old, rusty badge.

I remind myself, "There is no room in love for fear. Well-formed love banishes fear. Since fear is crippling, a fearful life—fear of death, fear of judgment—is one not yet fully formed in love" (1 John 4:18 MSG).

I'm not fully formed in love yet, but I continue to make more space and more room for love to banish fear.

Love banishes the old, rusty badge.

At this point in my own journey, I've begun to wonder if

everyone wants to be well, to be whole. It is a question I had to ask myself. I think of the cripple, in the Bible, at the pool of Bethesda. "When Jesus noticed him lying there [helpless], knowing that he had been *in that condition* a long time, He said to him, "Do you want to get well?" (John 5:6 AMP, emphasis added).

"Do you want to get well?" Jesus asks.

He had been in his condition for a long time, the story tells us. *Have you been in a broken condition for a long time? Spirit, soul, or body?*

It's easy to say, "Yes, I want to be whole; I want to be well." But it is another thing to mean it. To mean it so much that you subject yourself to change—allowing change to be done in you. Letting the work of removing and replacing begin and continue as many times as it takes. If we are not paying attention, we can become accustomed to our brokenness. One day we wake up and find it familiar like a ratty old bathrobe, and if we get too comfortable with it, over time it will become our identity; it becomes a badge. Worst of all, somewhere along the way we may begin to believe that it will always be this way; things will never change. We accept the badges of brokenness as part of our permanent customized menagerie.

I have walked this fine line to the point of believing "this is now who I am." And "this is how things will always be." I confess there are still days when the lies look more like truth because the circumstances paint that picture. And I recall so vividly, in the days when I felt hopeless, how the possibility of my heart being repaired or made whole was not a probability, in my mind, at all. I convinced myself that if I could manage and cope with my pain, then I could at least survive.

But Jesus keeps asking, *"Do you want to get well?"*

Now that I'm paying attention to what I'm shelving in my heart, allowing God to shine a light on the dark display, He has identified rejection front and center. Like an ugly old vase that is always empty and always crying out to be filled. It's been there so long, covered in cobwebs, that I never was able to see it for what it was. But I have no doubts now that rejection sits stoic, like a work of art, on my shelves grouped together with the bits and bobs it has acquired over the years: low self-esteem, people-pleasing, perfectionism, performing, fear of man, loneliness, self-protection, and self-rejection.

I see what sits on my shelf, and *I WANT to get well!*

Jesus knows I've been in this condition a long time. He gently removes rejection to replace it with acceptance.

"He *chose us* in Him before the foundation of the world, that we should be holy and without blame before Him in love, having *predestined us to adoption as sons (and daughters)* by Jesus Christ to Himself, according to the good pleasure of His will, to the praise of the glory of His grace, by which *He has made us accepted in the Beloved*" (Eph. 1:4-6 NKJV, emphasis added).

The Greek word for acceptance, according to Strong's Concordance, means "to receive." He was rejected that we could receive acceptance. This is the beauty of the finished work.

Being accepted in the Beloved shatters the cobweb-covered empty vase.

I now receive acceptance as a candelabrum that will display the light of healing that is taking place in me.

———— ....

There is beauty within the broken and in the process, Lovely One. We are learning to look for it, to notice it, to mine for it, and to be found by it. When you encounter Beauty Himself, you will be greeted with an invitation for transformation.

The question is, *"Do you want to get well?"*

———— ....

Tips on Styling Shelves

01 / Books or objects? You decide. Or be wild and mix both.

02 / Think about what story you want to tell. The places you've been. The people you love. The things that inspire you.

03 / Group books by color for cohesiveness and pretty pops of color.

04 / Add as many personal touches as possible: souvenirs from travels, art that has meaning, photographs that share your history and warm your heart.

05 / If you buy objects to fill in spaces, stick with one color (all-white pottery, for instance) or a common denominator like brass.

06 / Group objects in odd numbers. A pretty pairing might be two pieces of pottery with a succulent in front.

07 / Group your books by topic for easy access to share. If you think this is a hassle, you're right. If you do not, then I can bet you already do this or that it is at least on your to-do list.

08 / If your shelves need to be functional yet you still want them to be beautiful, consider buying decorative boxes to store unsightly things within like electronic cords and DVD and video game cases.

CHAPTER TWENTY-SEVEN | WHO YOU WILL ALWAYS BE

"As long as 'being the Beloved' is little more than
a beautiful thought or a lofty idea that hangs above
my life to keep me from becoming depressed, nothing
really changes. What is required is to become the Beloved
in the commonplaces of my daily existence and, bit by bit,
to close the gap between what I know myself to be and the
countless specific realities of everyday life."

—HENRI NOUWEN, *LIFE OF THE BELOVED*[1]

When I look in the mirror, here is what I see: a short little girl who grew gray hair and crow's feet. The pattern of lines on my face now more prominent than my familiar freckles. The bags under my eyes, the badge of brokenness, late-night baby feedings, and binge blogging. I wonder where I went. Because I feel somewhat unacquainted with the reflection I see.

If mirrors could reflect traits, character, and personality, would we be able to master the art of finding beauty within? This too, I'm certain, would be hard to see. We'd be squinting into our souls, trying to peer past every uncomely intimate quality.

Beauty in me?

It was a particularly harried weekend, in a most prickly way. I had to write a proposal on a book I wasn't planning to write yet was very intrigued by; my sweet in-laws were coming to town; we had a long-ago-scheduled dinner with friends at a favorite restaurant, which I wasn't about to cancel; and I had the Original Conference photo shoot on Sunday. I'm usually behind the camera, helping to direct and style, but this year I was also asked to be in the photos, and, well, I'm no good at saying no to friends. With that last detail, I convinced myself that I would have to cram driving sixty miles to the nearest Nordstrom to look for something suitable to wear into my already crazy schedule.

The Sunday afternoon of the shoot I was in the bathroom, curling my hair, when I received a text from my aunt. She wanted to let me know that they were putting my grandma on palliative care. I knew she wasn't doing great. Three months earlier, when I hugged her goodbye, I knew it very well could be the last visit, the last "look at you" embrace. But I felt like this had come from out of nowhere; there was no major illness or hospital stay. I reminded myself that I was several states away and I wasn't seeing how she fared and faded day to day. I didn't want to accept this development because I knew what hospice meant. I had lived through it, day to day, with my grandpa who lived only a few streets away.

I was on the brink of losing it, from the stress and from the anticipated loss—the relentless loss that wouldn't seem to leave me alone. I wasn't really sure how I was going to smile for the camera, let alone contain tears and keep my makeup on.

And so I showed up to the photo shoot, squeezed my eyes tight, blinked a lot, and turned to wipe tears when no one was looking. When I was behind the camera, I was in my element and busy enough to be distracted. When I was in front of it, I'd catch myself in a pensive stare, which Jen and Lisa would continually break by jumping in front of the cameras for a laugh. Eventually, I let myself be present and found beauty in our surroundings—the old brick wall chipping with gray paint (a perfect patina)—in my friends, in new acquaintances, in the purpose of Original, and in the work God gave me. It was what my grandma would have wanted, and anyway, she was always about getting the job done and done right.

Our last shooting location was in a field. It was sunset, and we had smoke bombs. We traipsed through bug-laden brush that was almost as tall as I was. I held the flowers that Lori had so effortlessly arranged, while both Jen and Lori crouched down behind me waving around pink smoke bombs and coughing. It was quite an ordeal. What looks ethereal and wistful was anything but in the moment.

I remember thinking, *What a beautiful shot.* Like an otherworldly scene where I played the part of a fairy—the sunset, the field, the flowers, the pink wisps of magic dancing through the summer sky. And then I returned to reality—*This is certainly not the real me. Maybe I'll write a blog or an essay about this very shot*, I thought. *I'll talk about how this is not real. How it is fun to pretend, but this is not the e-v-e-r-y-d-a-y.* The real me is often wearing the shirt I slept in, trying to decide if it is acceptable to go another day without washing my hair. The real me thinks to herself, *It's amazing what professional makeup, good photography, friends making you laugh, and smoke bombs can do.*

> WE ARE DYING IN OUR STRIVING,
> AND YET WE ARE STRIVING TO BE
> LESS THAN WHO WE REALLY ARE.

My sister Amy got ahold of the picture and got all poetic. She said, "Trina, *this* is who you really are." I laughed. Sometimes I don't take my Amy seriously. She is younger and a free spirit who initially makes responsibility rise up in me. But these days, I seem to come around to what she says. Being a free spirit is not just an idiom of birth order or personality. Her spirit truly is free in areas where mine still seems to be bound. So I'm learning to let her free spirit call out more freedom in me.

I look at the picture and, instead of looking closer to try to see what she sees, I hear. I hear the word *BELOVED.* I hear the word that I have tattooed on my arm, *BIEN-AIMÉ.* I hear what God sees.

Here is what God sees, e-v-e-r-y-d-a-y, when He looks at you and me—He sees His Beloved.

It has nothing to do with the mirror or the "me" I aspire or try to be. It only has to do with whom He calls me, "Beloved."

Lovely One, we are dying in our striving. And yet we are striving to be less than who we really are. Striving, working, chasing, earning, and proving will never transform us into who we want to be. *We are already what we long to be—loved.* We only have to shed who we are not. This isn't about personality or any kind of deficiency. This is about an unawareness of identity.

In working through the broken, giving God permission to enter all the rooms, forgotten or locked, so much ugly emerges (remember my anger, jealousy, bitterness, and unforgiveness). The things you never thought were in *you* surface, like cream rising to the top. This is when you feel so vulnerable, so ugly, so naked, so exposed. You will want to hide. You may not be able to even face yourself. Yet these moments are when I've most tangibly felt Jesus pursue me. Not to correct me but to lavish love upon me as a covering.

Like a dance, He extends and offers His hand. Because I reject myself, I many times reject Him too. Out of a twisted self-preservation, I decline; whether by my words or actions, I give Him my reasons and my rationalizations. Out of my fear of rejection, I reject Him.

He responds, "And *yet* you are so lovely."

Does He really call us lovely when we feel so dark, so weak, so worn out and washed up? When we are at our worst? When we turn our heads and hearts from Him?

"*Yet* you are so lovely."

The Shumalite's story, recorded thousands of years ago in Song of Songs, reads like a modern-day journal entry:

"I know I am so unworthy—so in need."

"*Yet* you are so lovely!"

"I feel as dark and dry as the desert tents of the wandering nomads."

"*Yet* you are so lovely."

This changes everything when we allow Him to tell us what He sees.

"Let me tell you how I see you. My dearest darling, you are so lovely! You are beauty itself to me" (Song of Songs 1:5, 9, 15 TPT).

When we are naked and bare, our perception is that the Light will feel too bright, too revealing: *What if I am burned*? Yet the Light's job is to reveal who we truly are: Loved by God. Loved by God at our best. Loved by God at our worst. As John called himself, "the one Jesus loved dearly" (John 13:23 MSG), so must we. The light does burn, Lovely One. It burns away the compulsion to focus on our imperfections and spotlights our warped view, giving us eyes to see that our identity is in the Perfect Love that lives in us.

WE ARE ALREADY WHAT WE LONG TO BE—LOVED.

We are trying to busy ourselves with work, activities, social causes, and every other thing in an effort either to work ourselves out of the person we don't want to be or to convince ourselves (and others) that there are still some good, some lovable qualities within. When likely all God is asking us to do is to slow down enough to listen. Maybe it's a forced hand by way of your circumstance or brokenness, as it was for me. Either way, He wants nothing but for us to sit with Him.

Sit with Him so that He can have a good look at you. Not to point out flaws, as you're accustomed to doing with yourself or as others have done to you. No, rather, He wants to sit with you and trace your belovedness.

Sitting still. Sitting quiet. Listening to the voice of acceptance. It's like the sound of the tide rolling in from the sea. It rolls in and out, and out and in, and never stops. Day and night, whispering...

Beloved.
Beloved.
Beloved.

Have you been busy your whole life boasting of your love for God, like Peter? Like me? Has the tide sound of your heart been...

I love God.
I love God.
I love God.

It's John who, more often, gets called out for boasting. I've heard so many sermons that take the mickey out of him for basically calling himself Jesus's favorite. But, Beloved, he was. John was Jesus's favorite; Peter was Jesus's favorite; I am, and so are you. Could it be that John knew this, believed it, because he is the one who rested his head on Jesus's chest? With his very own ears he heard the tide sound of Jesus's heart, and it sounded like this:

I love you, John.
I love you, John.
I love you, John.

Today, He wants to turn the tide. To go all elementary. To have us listen to the lullaby:

Yes, Jesus loves me.
Yes, Jesus loves me.
Yes, Jesus loves ME.[3]

My grandma Eleanor used to sing that old-timey song to J.J., Amy, and me in her soft, slightly raspy voice. I can hear her sound and still smell the mixed-sweet scent of perfumed Airspun powder, coffee cake, and after-dinner coffee. And she would hold us close to her heart when she sang. I know now that those words went to the deep places of my little-girl heart.

> ONLY WHEN WE ACCEPT OURSELVES
> AS BELOVED HAVE WE MASTERED
> THE ART OF FINDING BEAUTY WITHIN.

This past year I was on the treadmill listening to worship

from Bethel, attempting to take care of my body and allowing God to work in my heart. It was a spontaneous mix of songs, and somewhere in the middle they broke into "Jesus Loves Me," Sunday school–style. As I walked in the basement, at a speed of 3.0, the melody in my ears met the truth in the deep places of my little-girl heart and something broke—or rather was repaired—in me.

For almost a year, I had been studying about being the beloved—reading, listening, and researching. Yet it was when those familiar words were sung that the Light revealed who I had always been (but stopped believing along the way)—loved by God. And it burned away all I had covered myself in for the past thirty-five years.

Only when we accept ourselves as beloved have we mastered the art of finding beauty within. And, dare I say, only when we accept ourselves as beloved are we able to see, truly see, the beauty all around us. As Henri Nouwen says, "How can I search for beauty and truth unless that beauty and truth are already known to me in the depth of my heart?"[2]

This revelation of being "who I will always be" now goes beyond me. At night, I tuck the kids in, and after prayers I tell them they are God's beloved. Eventually after prayer I ask, "Who are you?"

"Beloved," they answer in the purest little munchkin voices.

"Who does God call you?"

My youngest yells out, "Rocco Beloved McBear." Apparently Rocco thought this was our last name, which also means he thought Beloved was his middle name.

I feel I have done my job as a mom if he keeps that name for the rest of his life. I don't want Rocco (or any of my children) to layer up in their own coverings, as they grow, disguising Beloved McBear. Inevitably they will. Because the world is cold and we reach for the nearest coat (or the ones given to us) rather than the one we already have. However, I'm comforted to know that beneath it all, there is the heartbeat tide of love; and when they tune in to the deep places of their little-boy or -girl hearts, they will see who they have always been and always will be—Beloved.

I look at this photo of me now and remember the details of the day. Mostly, it is a souvenir of the Spirit, which invited me to believe that this is how God sees me.

TWENTY-EIGHT

"Above all, watch with glittering eyes the whole world around you because the greatest secrets are always hidden in the most unlikely places. Those who don't believe in magic will never find it."

—ROALD DAHL, *THE MINPINS*[1]

Practice makes perfect, they say.

I've always wondered who "they" are. The "they"s in all of the "they say"s that we absorb and repeat, like robots. Have you wondered too? "They say it's a good idea to keep a blanket, coffee can, candle, and lighter in your car," my mom says, "in case you are stranded in a blizzard, that is."

Practice isn't about perfect, I say.

I don't know about you, but I've always thought of "practice" as a word that follows words like "piano" or "play," "football" or "track." All of my life I've seen it as a requirement, a necessity to play in a game or perform, a drudgery you were doomed to after school or before you could go out and play.

But these days I'm looking at practice in a whole new way, with fresh youthful eyes that don't need glasses to see clearly. I don't see it as a means to an end but rather a way, a road to take a walk on.

I've begun to look at beauty as a practice—in every sense of the definition, really. It's something I try to observe, follow with my eyes and life. It's become a habit, a custom. It's also an application, an exercise, a performance of activity as the Oxford dictionary would define it.[2]

I've been practicing my beholding.

Are you beginning to notice beauty? Grand or Lilliputian.

If you are beginning to behold, do you acknowledge it? Capture it or whisper thanks.

If you are acknowledging it, does it shape you? Soften your edges or draw new lines. Whitewash or color the gray.

There are days when I can't seem to find beauty, when my eyes are dull and my readers aren't providing any more clarity. On those days, the practice entails creating. The custom, on some days, becomes an activity.

Don't let the word "create" scare you, like running the mile frightened you enough to not go out for track. I never considered myself creative or artistic. I wasn't into coloring or crafting as a kid, other than an occasional afternoon with my Spirograph or Shrinky Dinks. Creating, for me, came in the form of conceiving pretend businesses and stores. I came up with ideas and then imagined myself the boss of my siblings or neighborhood friends, whoever would dare to play. I was so into creating these entities that at one slumber party I put together a post office, complete with packages (Spanish Bibles we brought home from church to send to Colombia) and an assembly line. I was having a great time, but apparently my fifth-grade guests were not. One of them—Kristie, I think—snuck off from my watch and went and told my mom they didn't want to play anymore or, more likely, they didn't want to work. My mom made her way down to the basement with a bag of M&M's and a VHS and said it was movie time. I remember telling her that I didn't think anyone wanted to watch a movie because we were all having so much fun playing post office. Clearly, I was probably the only one. Sorry, my fifth-grade friends.

I went on to junior high to find out that I was terrible in art class, previously believing that I was more left-brained than right. In high school I liked creative writing but oddly enough never thought of it as "creative." And yet, between 1995 and now, I've done a lot of creating, most of the time without realizing it could be labeled as that.

The question is not whether we are creative. The question is: How will you, personally, express beauty?

God expressed His beauty through all of creation. It came in sunsets and colors and in you and me. We are all children of the Creator, and thus creating is in our genes. It's easy for me to think of God as the Creator. I've known Him as creating the earth, Adam and Eve, the beginning—since my own. But I don't often think about what that must have looked like. Who could ever fully imagine? But when I read Genesis 1 and Proverbs 8 and allow myself to visualize a great nothing, suddenly the whole world, the one He's got in His hands, becomes so much more than a story I was told at my beginning. It is the cool turquoise reality I dip my toes in on vacation and all of the tiny, sand-covered shells, twenty different varieties, I bring back with me. It is the snowcapped mountains I drive my rental car right through while visiting family out West. It is the roadside quartz I pack between shoes in my suitcase.

Did you know that when the earth was created, it wasn't just God the Father at work? Jesus was there too. "I was there, close to the Creator's side as his master artist" (Prov. 8:30 TPT).

I've known Jesus to be there at the beginning (according to John 1:1). But to think of Him at the Creator's side as a master artist? That opened up a whole new understanding in me.

Before the oceans depths were poured out,
and before there were any glorious fountains
overflowing with water,
I was there, dancing!
Even before one mountain had been sculpted
or one hill raised up,
I was already there, dancing!
When he created the earth, the fields,

even the first atom of dust,
I was already there.
When he hung the tapestry of the heavens
and stretched out the horizon of the earth,
when the clouds and skies were set in place
and the subterranean fountains began to flow strong,
I was already there.
When he set in place the pillars of the earth
and spoke the decrees of the seas,
commanding the waves
so that they wouldn't overstep their boundaries,
I was there, close to the Creator's side as his master artist.
(Proverbs 8:24–30 TPT, emphasis added)

This is the one who makes His home in your heart. You, Lovely One, are housing a master artist.

Thus, it's not a matter of *if* we are creative; it's a matter of *how.*

Will you create beauty through your words, with paint, through a hug, in color, by cooking, by the click of a camera, a timely word, a full-tooth smile, or helping a friend in need? The expression of beauty can take many forms and finds its way out, uniquely, in you.

It turns out I express beauty through writing and ideas, as I've always done (minus the bossing around). This is how I create. This is my practice. It's what I return to, and it's what I turn to when everything goes dark and my eyes feel blinded to beauty. Many times, it's the channel in which Beauty Himself finds me—over and over as many times as I need finding.

The practice of beauty is a ministry—it is recognizing and accepting the offerings of the Creator and in turn creating something beautiful to offer to others. It's fully living as a child created in the image of God. It's allowing the master artist to open the windows in the home of your heart and let His light shine out, coloring the dark places in your life and ultimately the lives of those you encounter. This, in turn, is an offering of thanksgiving given back to Him.

YOU, LOVELY ONE, ARE HOUSING A MASTER ARTIST. THUS, IT'S NOT A MATTER OF *IF* WE ARE CREATIVE; IT'S A MATTER OF *HOW*.

From Him to you and you to me. From Him to me and me to you. And so the offering never ends.

This kind of practice is not a work. It is not something to strive for or aim to be perfect at. Practice doesn't make perfect. God is not looking for perfect anyway. In fact, He is looking to free us from the confines of perfectionism. Perfectionism chokes out creativity. It keeps our God-given gifts wrapped up, tied up, and tucked away somewhere deep within, with the windows shut. It robs us from living fully in His image.

Is it that we believe because God is perfect, we must be too, or is it that we fear if we are less than, we will not be loved or even noticed? Maybe a little of both. When we live this way, we do one of two things: we either choke the life out of ourselves in our striving, or, perhaps even sadder, we do nothing at all. I've often wondered if those who have been labeled "lazy" are more afraid of failure than they are of hard work.

The measure of love we receive is never determined by the quality or consistency of what we do. The measure of love that is available has to do only with what Jesus has already done—and the supply is immeasurable. You may be accustomed to working your fingers to the bone in order for a significant person in your life to approve of or applaud you, but people-pleasing doesn't work with God. Trust me, I've tried.

THE MEASURE OF LOVE WE RECEIVE IS NEVER DETERMINED BY THE QUALITY OR CONSISTENCY OF WHAT WE DO. THE MEASURE OF LOVE THAT IS AVAILABLE HAS TO DO ONLY WITH WHAT JESUS HAS ALREADY DONE—AND THE SUPPLY IS IMMEASURABLE.

These days, I call myself a recovering perfectionist. The scales have finally fallen off my eyes, and I see how enslaved I'd been by perfectionism, people-pleasing, performing, and proving. Of course, I would have told you that I wasn't perfect. Who is? I would have said I didn't even *strive* for perfection. But my body would have told you otherwise— headaches, stomachaches, and body shakes. Maybe my mind was in denial to call it what it was: nothing short of exhausting myself, head to toe, in trying to get as close to good enough as possible. I call myself "recovering" because the truth is I revert. I put it down and pick it back up. I fall back into years of "If I do this, then will they be proud of me?" "If I don't do that, will they be mad at me?" "If I do more, will I receive more love?" The thing is I now not only feel the weight when I return to it, I can see it for what it truly is. And I can see it doesn't serve God or me well.

When God created the earth, He saw all that He made and said that it was "good." I wonder why He didn't say "perfect." When I create, whether with words or by the story of my life, I'm trying, like my Father, to say it is "good."

On days when I don't have the time to create, I make my practice about observing. I keep my eyes, ears, and heart wide open to the everyday ordinary beauty. I make a habit not to skip around it but live in all of the moments. I appreciate what I used to look past. The ordinary everyday is not trying to take my time; it has something to offer. For the longest time I boxed "beautiful" into trips and oceans, birthdays and confetti. But ordinary is just as beautiful. It's Cinderella in her work clothes. *Can you see?* Remember; don't discount your ordinary moments, Lovely One, because these are the moments we were made for. And anyway, the ball gown, pumpkin carriage, and glass slipper would become very ordinary if you were in them every day.

Through the beginning of my brokenness I couldn't see any of it, work clothes or ball gown. Seeing didn't even seem like a possibility; my eyes were clouded with tears and movies of memories. I was in survival mode. It's a horrible place to live. Eventually I found that when we go from survival to surrender, we go from broken to whole. If you are able to fine-comb the bad times and feel it all...you have the same capacity to fine-comb the good and feel it all, even if you are somewhere smack dab in the middle of broken and whole. This past year, I can honestly say finding beauty in the everyday really has become a practice I have not perfected.

I practice noticing the bleeding-pink colors of the sunset and the bleeding shades of blue in Luke's eyes. I practice saying thank you when I enter the grocery store that still happens to bring up bad emotions in me; when I'm there I regard the ombre shading of the pink lady apples and whisper, "Thank you that I am able to choose them." I practice writing words when I feel sad and also when I feel happy. I practice listening to the sound, fluctuation, and tone of the voices of the ones I love—soon changing with age—the same as the tune, the wave, the breeze of the trees. I practice looking at my soft stomach in the shower and remember the beauty of growing four children, each so different yet looking very much the same. I practice meeting my reflection in the mirror and seeing whom God sees.

THE ORDINARY EVERYDAY IS NOT TRYING TO TAKE MY TIME; IT HAS SOMETHING TO OFFER.

I'm not good at doing this every day, but the true art, you see, is returning to the practice. Noticing. Expressing. Creating. Return and repeat.

When we go from
survival to surrender,
we go from
broken to whole
♡

CHAPTER TWENTY-NINE | A FULL LIFE IN THE
EMPTIEST OF PLACES

fe in
ptiest
es

TWENTY-NINE

*"For it is only in the emptiness that comes
from parting with what we have that
divine fullness can flow in."*

—ANDREW MURRAY, *ABIDING IN CHRIST*[1]

omewhere in the beginning of my brokenness, I put
this passage in my pocket:

I'll give you a full life in the emptiest of places—
    firm muscles, strong bones.
You'll be like a well-watered garden,
    a gurgling spring that never runs dry.
(Isaiah 58:11 MSG)

I tucked this "full life in the emptiest of places" promise
away in my pocket, but it wanted to find a home in the barren parts of my heart.

It sounded like something to find or seek: a full life. It was strange to think of full when I felt so empty, so depleted, so turned upside down and shaken out, like pennies from a pocket.

The more I looked at the string of words, I noticed that it wasn't a promise to fix everything, to restore things back to how they were, to repair them to be better than before. Rather, it's a guarantee of a gift—"I'll give you," it says. I read again: "In the emptiest of places, I will *give* you a full life."

From pocket to the heart I began to believe in the possibility of a full life. Not after all was mended or a new normal was achieved. Not when I "felt" full. No—right in the middle of the empty, I could be full. The loss. The broken. The break. A *full* life. A well-watered garden. A spring that never runs dry.

⸻ ....

This past summer as I was staring at the pool in our backyard—a deep, once-empty space now filled with water—I heard the voice of Love whisper: *Emptiness is simply a thing that I fill. I will fill the deep, empty ends with my love. The deeper the end, the more love to pour in.*

When I look at the pool I don't see it empty, I see it full. The water is what makes it beautiful, peaceful. The water is what makes it useful, gives it a purpose. The water is what beckons others to come. To relax. To play. To be refreshed.

The whisper went on: *Do not focus on the empty spaces,*

Dear Heart. Focus on how I am filling them. You are so focused on the empty. On lack. On others that you look to to fill. But do not focus there. Remind yourself that empty allows more room for Me to pour My love, My living water, into. It's time to swim into My fullness. I can't say this means a season of everything fixed. A season of everything feeling the way you want it to. Rather, you will learn to feel full in Me, no matter what your circumstances. And no one can empty the water of My Word, except for you.

Fill up on the words I speak to you and have already spoken. Over and over again. Drink deeply, letting My living water fill the deep places in you. When I was baptized, plunged under into the deep, these were the words that filled me: "This is my beloved Son, with whom I am well pleased."

Out of His fullness we are filled.

"And now out of his fullness we are fulfilled! And from him we receive grace heaped upon grace!" (John 1:16 TPT).

Out of His fullness we are fulfilled.

The gift of a full life is offered. Will you receive?

It begins by making peace with coming up short and resigning to no longer toil to fill the emptiness and not-enoughness on our own. We have to stop rationalizing for how deep or shallow our ends are and stop apologizing for not doing enough or being enough—for He is more than enough.

This is the beauty of not enough.

Two years ago, things were at an all-time low. I was empty upon empty, after seeing a light at the end of a very dark tunnel abruptly snuffed out. For several weeks I felt like I had been through a literal battle that was fought around the clock. The experience was traumatic (it still, to this day, is difficult for me to replay the details in my mind). When the outcome was not what I had prayed for, fought for (in action and prayer), and hoped desperately for, I was in a state of shock. I ended up spending a day in bed, exhausted, and, frankly, very depressed. I spent two weeks in a stupor with only enough energy and mental capacity to play Candy Crush, watch movies, and sit by the fire with my family.

OUT OF HIS FULLNESS WE ARE FILLED. OUT OF HIS FULLNESS WE ARE FULFILLED.

Yet this is when I discovered that the beauty of not enough is where you'll find all that you need.

Somewhere between crushing candy and the Empire striking back, I was brought back, again, to Isaiah 58. Only this time I dug a little deeper in my pocket and read a little further.

I'll give you a full life in the emptiest of places—
	firm muscles, strong bones.
You'll be like a well-watered garden,
	a gurgling spring that never runs dry.

You'll use the old rubble of past lives to build anew,
    rebuild the foundations from out of your past.
You'll be known as those who can fix anything,
    restore old ruins, rebuild and renovate,
    make the community livable again.
(Isaiah 58:11–12 MSG)

This time I saw not only the promise of being filled but what precedes the promise: building.

Empty begets full. Broken begets building.

Broken is the place where He builds. And the pieces of our broken heart, our broken lives, the destruction, and the rubble are never wasted; they are used to build anew.

And again, this work is a collaboration. He restores, and in the process we become restorers.

THE BEAUTY OF NOT ENOUGH IS WHERE YOU'LL FIND ALL THAT YOU NEED.

During that dark December, in the middle of my stupor, wearing pajamas all hours of the day, the Father showed me that my broken pieces, the rubble of my life, would be used to help rebuild the lives of others. I believe He is showing you, even now, maybe in your pajamas, that the broken pieces, the rubble of your life, will be used to help others rebuild. From the foundations of our past, brick upon brick, rubble upon rubble, comes restoration.

I couldn't get past the thread of it all. The broken home that broke me, the rebuilding, the call to become a restorer of homes. I would have never seen this trajectory, but God did. He sees the beginning from the end and the end from the beginning. "Repairer of the Breach, Repairer of Broken Walls, Restorer of Homes, Restorer of Dwellings" (Isa. 58, several translations). This is my life's calling, given to me in a most empty place. Filled and fulfilled.

What is it that you are called to repair or restore?

———— ....

It's been a good few years since the lowest low and the Candy Crush and the calling. There have been plenty of ups and downs, emptying and filling, since. Together we are still renovating, rebuilding, and restoring. And the beauty of not enough has filled my every days, the deep ends and shallows.

For me, a "full life in the emptiest of places" has looked a little bit like:

A regular Monday night doing the dishes, only I'm having a kitchen dance party rather than staring out the window lost in sorrow and worry.

Giving thanks when there is much to complain about.

Hearing the faint song of the bird through the wind and the rain.

Being emptied, to be filled, to be emptied, to be filled.

Binding up the brokenhearted with a hug, a meal, a coat, or a kind word.

Feeling it *all*! The pain so I can feel the joy. The joy so I can work through the pain.

Intentionally adding more laughter. By friends. By movies. By acting silly like I used to.

Spending time sitting in the presence of God without any agenda but to be still and listen.

Taking chances I never would have taken before because I'm beginning to see beyond the past and I have vision for the days to come.

Trusting like a child, not concerned about tomorrow or next week.

Looking for others to encourage when I could use the encouragement myself.

Hoping against hope but not fixating on the outcome, leaving the how and when to God.

Doing something with all my hurt, heartbreak, and pain instead of letting it be the reason I don't do anything.

A full life looks like grace heaped upon grace.

CONCLUSION | KISS OF THE SON

CONCLUSION

"How does the Meadow-flower its bloom unfold?
Because the lovely little flower is free
Down to its root, and, in that freedom, bold;"
—WILLIAM WORDSWORTH, "A POET! HE HATH PUT HIS HEART TO SCHOOL"

I am away writing at a house in the trees. It is so lovely here. I count it a gift, and I am grateful. But sitting right next to this gift is grief. At least this morning. It's Saturday, and looking outside you can feel it's the weekend. It appears as if the air is on holiday. I think it actually is. It's February, and I'm told the temperature is sixty degrees. How strange. As strange as the way I feel.

It's as if I woke up and grief was jealous of gratitude. It was jealous of grace. I feel it got ample attention yesterday when its tide washed over me and the waves of not having my grandma hit, pulling me under, with a howl and groan, whipping me about in *all* that has been lost. I find gratitude, again, for what was. I breathe in Grace. But here is loss again—listing, listing, listing—begging for me to listen. I start my own listing—thanks, thanks, thanks.

This place is so peaceful. Trees. Lakes. Rest and retreat. It feels like a parenthesis from the everyday. The views give me perspective and let me see peace with my eyes.

I've been watching flocks of geese fly by in formation. They are coming from the blue lake beyond. I ponder where they are going. Leaving beauty. Who am I to know their direction, which way the wind blows, or their destination? I think of the geese in my town that gather in groups to cross the street of dirty, slushy snow, babies waddling behind, only to sit in a boggy retention pond across from McDonald's.

DON'T LEAVE THE LAKE! I will them a telepathic rebuke.

I wonder if the ones in the middle that haven't led in front yet—or have already moved to the back—even have a clue to the way they are headed. Maybe near McDonald's or maybe north? I imagine them heading north. I picture them flying over the Canadian Rockies, over Banff and the historic castle-like hotel I wish to visit one day, and landing in the aqua waters of Lake Louise.

From beauty to beauty.

They float in the Canadian lake that looks as if it is embraced by majesty. Yet, come winter, they won't think twice when it's time to leave.

I think to myself, *I just want to live in and around created beauty.* And the Spirit whispers, *There is still so much your eyes do not see.*

It is March. To my surprise, I woke up to a blanket of snow clothing the earth and large twirling snowflakes dancing in the workday air. No one I know is a fan of snow in March, but I am away writing at the tree house again, and I can't say I mind. As the flakes turned to flurries and the clouds were moody and moving about, the sun began to shine. Snow and sun. Winter welcoming spring.

The tulips will be returning soon. The Dutch ruby reds and sunshine yellows. The very ones I told my children the fairies sleep in (I wish they still believed). The same fairies I daydreamed of being so that I could fly away from the everyday. I saw those yellow and reds as rest and retreat and a way to flee. I realize now that I have been in my own kind of cocoon. Quiet. Receiving. Wrestling. Growing. Allowing the empty places to be filled.

Winter is coming to an end.

And the fragrance of the flower is whispering, over you, over me...

Now he comes closer,
even to the places where I hide.
He gazes into my soul,
peering through the portal

As he blossoms within my heart.
The one I love calls to me:

Arise, my dearest. Hurry, my darling.
Come away with me!
I have come as you have asked
to draw you to my heart and *lead you out.*
For now is the time, my beautiful one.
The season has changed,
the bondage of your barren winter has ended,
and the season of hiding is over and gone.
The rains have soaked the earth
and left it bright with blossoming flowers.
The season for singing and pruning the vines has arrived.
I hear the cooing of doves in our land,
filling the air with songs to awaken you
and guide you forth.
Can you not discern this new day of destiny
breaking forth around you?
The early signs of my purposes and plans
are bursting forth.
The budding vines of new life
are now blooming everywhere.
The fragrance of their flowers whispers,
"There is change in the air."
Arise, my love, my beautiful companion,
and run with me to the higher place.
For now is the time to arise and come away with me.
(Song of Songs 2:9–13 TPT, emphasis added)

He has led me out of my hiding place; the tulip has opened to the kiss of the Son, and I, like the fairies, have been set free.

All that I wished and prayed to be restored was not. But I was.

All ends are a beginning.

All death is new life.

All beauty is found in each and every day.

THE END

Your beauty and love chase after me
every day of my life.

(PSALM 23:6 MSG)

ENDNOTES

1. C. S. Lewis, *Till We Have Faces* (Orlando, FL: Harcourt Brace & Company, 1956/1980)

Introduction
1. John Eldredge and Stasi Eldredge, *Captivating* (Nashville, TN: Thomas Nelson, 2005, 2010)

Chapter 1: The Offering of Beauty
1. Sue Monk Kidd, *Firstlight, The Early Inspirational Writings* (New York, NY: Penguin Group, 2006)
2. "Behold," Vocabulary.com, https://www.vocabulary.com /dictionary/behold
3. "Behold," Wiktionary, https://en.wiktionary.org/wiki/behold

Chapter 2: The End Is The Beginning
1. Louis L'Amour, *Lonely on the Mountain* (Bloomington, IN: AuthorHouse, 2016)
2. Rainer Maria Rilke, *Sonnets to Orpheus* (New York, NY: W. W. Norton & Company, Inc., 1942, 1970)

Chapter 3: The Landscape of a Broken Heart
1. William Shakespeare, *Measure for Measure* (Washington, DC: The Folger Shakespeare Library, 1997)
2. Matthew Wilder, *Break My Stride* (Private-I Records, 1983)
3. Henry Rollins, "Iron and the Soul," RossTraining.com (blog), December 4, 2009, http://rosstraining.com/blog/2009/12/04/

iron-and-the-soul-by-henry-rollins/. Essay was originally published in *Details* magazine in 1994.

Chapter 4: The Lived-In and Living Home

1. C. S. Lewis, *Mere Christianity* (New York, NY: Harper Collins, 1952, 1972)

Chapter 5: Look for a Lovely Thing

1. "Flânerie," found: https://en.wikipedia.org/wiki/Fl%C3%A2neur
2. Sainte-Beuve, found: https://en.wikipedia.org/wiki/Fl%C3%A2neur *"Grand dictionnaire universel,"* vol. 8, v. *flâneur* and *flânerie*

Chapter 7: A Change of Scenery

1. Anne Lamott, *Small Victories* (New York, NY: Riverhead Books, 2014)

Chapter 8: On Mental Clutter

1. J. M. Barrie, *Peter Pan* (New York, NY: Millennium Publications, 1911)
2. Emily Dickinson, "If Your Nerve, Deny You"

Chapter 10: Disconnectedly Connected

1. Dom Hubert Van Zeller, *We Die Standing Up* (Garden City, NY: Doubleday, 1949)
2. "Feel," Dictionary.com, http://www.dictionary.com/browse /feel?s=t
3. Phaedrus, found: https://www.goodreads.com/author /show/889.Phaedrus

Chapter 11: The Color of Soul Stretching

1. "Why Do We Not List Black and White as Colors in Physics?" seattlepi.com, http://education.seattlepi.com/not-list-black -white-colors-physics-3426.html and "Are Black & White

Colors?" Color Matters, https://www.colormatters.com/
color-and-design/are-black-and-white-colors

Chapter 12: What the Trees Tell Me

1. Mary Oliver, *When I Am Among the Trees* (Boston, MA: Beacon Press, 2006)
2. "Psithurism," The Free Dictionary, http://www.thefreedictionary.com/psithurism
3. "How Do Trees Survive Winter Cold?" Northern Woodlands, http://northernwoodlands.org/outside_story/article/tree-survive-winter-cold

Chapter 14: A Messy House and Life

1. Mary Randolph Carter, *A Perfectly Kept House Is the Sign of a Misspent Life* (New York, NY: Rizzoli International Publications, 2010)

Chapter 15: Milk Chocolate, If I Must

1. "Oasis," Oxford English Dictionary: https://en.oxforddictionaries.com/definition/Oasis

Chapter 16: On Friendship

1. Joseph Parry, Composer, *New Friends and Old Friends*, in Patricia S. Klein, *Random House Treasury of Friendship Poems* (New York, NY, Random House, 2006)

Chapter 17: Jumping Out of an Airplane, Almost

1. David Grayson, *Adventures in Solitude* (Frederick, CO: Renaissance House Publishers, 1990)
2. Robert Tew Quotes, Goodreads, https://www.goodreads.com/author/quotes/13848712.Robert_Tew
3. Susie Davis, *Unafraid: Trusting God in an Unsafe World* (Colorado Springs, CO: WaterBrook Press, 2015)

Chapter 18: Hanging Up (and Hung Up) on Memories

1. Jodi Picoult, *Vanishing Acts* (New York, NY: Washington Square Press, 2005)
2. Bette Midler, *Wind Beneath My Wings* (Atlantic Records, 1989)
3. "highly sensitive," found: http://hsperson.com/
4. A. R. Asher, Instagram, https://www.instagram.com/a.r.asher /?hl=en
5. Beau Taplin, Getaway. Found: http://afadthatlastsforever.tumblr .com/post/144557524327/a-memory-can-be-a-marvellous -getaway-but-you-must
6. Christopher Cross, *Sailing* (Warner Brothers, 1980)

Chapter 19: Coloring Their Days

1. Katie Morton, *The Secret Keeper* (New York, NY: Washington Square Press, 2012)

Chapter 20: On Acceptance

1. Cheryl Strayed, *Tiny Beautiful Things* (New York, NY: Vintage Books, 2012)
2. Reinhold Niebuhr, *Serenity Prayer*, Wikipedia, https://en.wikipedia .org/wiki/Serenity_Prayer
3. Janet Ungless, "Kris Carr's Crazy Sexy Anniversary," *Prevention*, February 4, 2013, https://www.prevention.com/mind-body /emotional-health/kris-carrs-crazy-sexy-cancer-anniversary

Chapter 21: DIY Your Life

1. Leo Tolstoy, Words and Quotes, http://www.wordsandquotes .com/quote/true-life-is-lived-when-tiny-changes-occur-leon -tolstoi-4992
2. Andrew Murray, *Abiding in Christ* (Minneapolis, MN: Bethany House, 2003)

Chapter 22: On Finding Your Style Self
1. Anne Morrow Lindbergh, *Gift from the Sea* (New York, NY: Pantheon Books, 1955)

Chapter 23: On Self-Care
1. A. A. Milne, *Winnie-the-Pooh* (New York, NY: Dutton Children's Books, 1926)

Chapter 24: Heaven Knows
1. Archilbad Henderson, *George Bernard Shaw: His Life and Works* (London: Hurst and Blackett, 1911)

Chapter 25: The Soul of a Home
1. Kate Morton, *The Secret Keeper* (New York, NY: Washington Square Press, 2012)
2. "Gezelligheid," Wikipedia, https://en.wikipedia.org/wiki/Gezelligheid
3. Anna Altman, "The Year of Hygge, the Danish Obsession with Getting Cozy," *The New Yorker,* December 18, 2016, http://www.newyorker.com/culture/culture-desk/the-year-of-hygge-the-danish-obsession-with-getting-cozy

Chapter 26: The Story on Your Shelves
1. Maya Angelou: Angelou's Facebook (2011) via *USA Today*: https://www.usatoday.com/story/news/nation-now/2014/05/28/maya-angelou-quotes/9663257/
2. Strong's Concordance: http://biblehub.net/searchstrongs.php?q=acceptance

Chapter 27: Who You Will Always Be
1. Henri J. M. Nouwen, *Life of the Beloved* (The Crossroad Publishing Company, 1992)
2. Ibid.

3. Anna Bartlett Warner, "Jesus Loves Me," 1860: https://en.wikipedia .org/wiki/Jesus_Loves_Me

Chapter 28: Practice Doesn't Make Perfect
1. Roald Dahl, *The Minpins* (New York, NY: Puffin Books, 1991)
2. "practice," found: https://en.oxforddictionaries.com/definition /practice

Chapter 29: A Full Life in the Emptiest of Places
1. Andrew Murray, *Abiding in Christ* (Minneapolis, MN: Bethany House, 2003)

Illustrations by: Camby Designs: pages 93, 113, 138–139, 155, 322

Photo Courtesy of City First Church, Original Women's Conference: pages 350–351

Trina McNeilly: pages 100–101, 103, 164–165, 302, 304

p. 309 photographer Amy Tompkins (photography owned by Trina McNeilly)

p. 310 photograph owned by Patricia Van Til

Photography by: Matthew Sandberg: pages 30–31, 126–127, 174–175, 187, 197, 207, 226–227, 232–233, 271, 276, 280–281, 292–293, 331, 336–337

Photography by: Yazy Jo: pages 71, 72–73, 74, 75, 246, 247, 248–249

ACKNOWLEDGMENTS

I t is my prayer that this book is an offering of beauty. Long before and during the penning, there were many who offered so much beauty, love, and support, and for that I am eternally grateful.

Many thanks to my agent, Angela Scheff. Thank you for taking a chance on me. You have been an advocate, guide, and kindred.

Thanks also to Christopher Ferebee for his wise counsel and for connecting me with Angela.

Many thanks to Keren Baltzer, my editor, for noticing beauty from the beginning, connecting with the heart of this project, and making allowance for creative freedom.

Thank you also to the entire team at FaithWords/Hachette.

Much gratitude to Aaron Campbell for his stellar artistry and for being able to tangibly translate and create, on a moment's notice, the imagery in my mind. You have been a sounding board on this project, and I'm grateful.

Thanks to Matthew Sandberg. Your great attention to color and detail make your photos that much more beautiful. It's always fun to collaborate.

Love and thanks to Lori Eickhoff for your shared love of beauty, creative eye, and speed styling. Thanks for always being my partner in design crime.

Thank you also to Photography by: Yazy Jo for taking photos of my home and family that capture the heart of our lived-in home. I'll treasure these forever.

Darcy and Dennis Staaland, thank you for allowing me write at your tree house. I felt such rest and retreat there.

Thanks to ABLE and the Land of Nod for adding beauty to my photos and my life over the years.

If this book had a theme song, it would be *Here Now* by Hillsong United. I started almost every writing session with that song as my prayer. Also in my ears: Bethel, Helen Jane Long, the *Amélie* soundtrack, Martin Smith, and Sleeping at Last, to name a few.

To my lovely blog readers: You are kindreds out looking for the lovely, waiting to be found by beauty. Thank you for noticing and for community.

Thank you, kindhearted Erin Loechner, for Voxing.

To dear ones who read through this book at various stages, offering insight and encouragement: Cindy Tompkins, Amy Tompkins, Erin Campbell, Michelle Weygandt, Christina Bacino, Jenny Ostrowski, Jessica Obee, Angela Scheff.

To friends who helped me in practical and thoughtful ways, such as praying, bringing over dinner, helping to watch and drive around my many children, or sending me memes of Ryan Gosling: Anna-Lisa Horton, Kendell Larson, Wendy Owens, Lindsay Tompkins, Michelle Weygandt, Stacey Welch.

Team Brave: Jen, Lisa, Lori, Liz. Thank you for all the prayers. The texts. The cheering. The making me jump out of an airplane, almost. However, I'm crossing this one off my list. #OTB

Girlfriends who have lived between the lines of this story, offering prayers and a listening ear. Thank you for sharing in tears, tea, cheeseburgers, and trips: Rebekah Lyons, Jen DeWeerdt, Maggie Sullivan, Christina Bacino, Anna-Lisa Horton, and Jill Johnson.

Pat Van Til, my aunt, for playing the part of the courier and also wise counselor. Every book you packaged up and took to the post office has been a brick in the foundation of my wholeness.

Much love and gratitude to my pastors and lifelong friends, Jeremy and Jen DeWeerdt. Jeremy, I would not be who I am today if it wasn't for you mentoring me as a teenager. I am forever grateful for your guidance, influence, and big broth-erness in my life. Jen, your becoming has been a guiding light. Thank you for being a cheering friend who has been there making me laugh through some of life's most difficult moments. I love you both dearly. You are family.

Much love and gratitude to my dear friends Gabe and Rebekah Lyons. For as long as I have known you two, you have been nudging me into who I was meant to be.

Thank you both for making me walk the tightrope (literally, Gabe), for taking me into your tiny NYC apartment when I needed to get away, for always including me and also connecting me with the right people at the right time. Rebekah, this book wouldn't be if it weren't for you. Thank you for calling out brokenness and greatness in me—at the same time—and for being a friend I can share my true self and heart with. I'm grateful God joined our paths all those years ago at INJOY. I love you both dearly. You are forever friends.

To my McNeilly family: Dave, Martha, Memaw, Scott, and Shea, Clint, and Angela Nowery (also my awesome nieces and nephews). Thank you for your many prayers, words of encouragement, and overwhelming kindness. I love you all.

Grandma, I'm believing there are books in heaven and that you are able to hold this in your hands (at least your favorite book about heaven tells me it's likely). I hope you find some lines worthy of a red pen underline. This is for you, Jeep. Your life was hard, but your brokenness was a seed into the soil of my life and so many others.

J.J. and Amy: My story is your story. Unmooring is scary, but we were created to sail the seas. You two have colored all my stories. I love you always, and...we will always have Red Lobster! Amy, my chief creative consultant, thank you for encouraging me, calling out creativity in me, listening to me, and being my personal prayer line. I carry your heart in my heart, sister.

Dad, I have you to thank for the ink in my veins. You gave

me a love for the written word. Word in print and the Word of God. I watched you day in and day out study, work hard, build, and be a person of great discipline. Thank you for instilling those qualities in me. I am forever grateful for the time you spent teaching me how to study, meditate, and speak God's Word.

Mom, you were my first vision of beauty. Still, you hold the spot of beauty personified. Even through all the brokenness you have managed to become more beautiful. I have no doubt that it is because of your love for God and His Word (Ps. 103:5). You have encouraged me to find beauty *in* the broken and the everyday, many times by example. Your unconditional love, encouragement, and practical help are the hands that help me to win.

To my wild, lovely brood, the ones who I am at home with:

Thank you, Ella, for your beautiful heart—wise beyond its years—and for helping me pick the right photo, always. Luke, for your hugs—they hold me together. Liam, for your empathy and wise little words. Rocco Beloved McBear— when I look at you, I understand what it means to be Beloved.

Stephen, the love of my life, I'll never forget the day you entered my story nor the day it became our story. It's you who is teaching me to write the future—to see the best before us rather than behind us. This book is very much yours. I couldn't have completed it without you! Thank you for being generous and making it possible for me to get away when needed (for survival or seeking words). Watching you love and enjoy our children is *beauty I notice* every single day. You are my hero! I love you for always.

Jesus, my home, the air that I breathe, my beginning, my end, my everything. Thank you for allowing me to spill out into this sacred story (Ps. 45:1 TPT).

Author: Trina McNeilly
Photo Credit: Matthew Sandberg

In 2008, Trina began authoring a popular lifestyle blog, La La Lovely. It became a place to work out her words and share inspiration—inspiration found sometimes in perfectly decorated spaces and other times in the broken places. Her work includes design and decorating projects, brand collaboration, art direction, and freelance writing.

Trina has written for online sites, including The Equals Record, Clementine Daily, Original Conference blog, Euro Style Lighting, Houzz, Kirtsy, and the Land of Nod blog. Trina has been featured in/on *The New York Times*, *Design Mom: How to Live with Kids*, the Land of Nod catalog, AOL.com, All Parenting, Apartment Therapy, and Style Me Pretty Living.

While Trina has done a lot of writing on the topic of decorating homes, her true passion is helping to bring the message of finding our home in the person of Jesus. Her heart's desire is to introduce others to the love of the Father. Through Him we find our identity and a full life that can start in even the emptiest of places.

Connect with Trina on Instagram and Twitter at @trina_mcneilly and on Facebook at @lalalovelyblog, where she shares beauty in the everyday, favorite finds, and encouraging words. Visit trinamcneilly.com for more stories and to join the conversation.